This Book Belongs To

FACES OF
RAP MOTHERS

Published in the United States of America

BEAT DEEP BOOKS

www.donnaink.shop | *www.donnaink.net*

CANDY STROTHER DEVORE-MITCHELL

Where Hip-Hop Meets Herstory.

NOMINATED

"2019's Most Entertaining Hip-Hop Book"

SOUL CENTRAL MAGAZINE

FACES OF RAP MOTHERS

FACES OF
RAP MOTHERS

BY

CANDY STROTHER DEVORE MITCHELL

Beat Deep Books Imprint
An imprint of **DonnaInk Publications, L.L.C.**
17611 Aquasco Road
Brandywine, MD 20613

BEAT DEEP BOOKS

Library of Congress Cataloging-in-Publication: 2019947579.
Mitchell, Candy Strother DeVore, author. Quesinberry, Donna, ghostwriter w/credit.
  Title: "Faces of Rap Mothers" / Candy Strother DeVore-Mitchell.
  220 p. cm.
      Subjects: BIO004000-BIOGRAPHY & AUTOBIOGRAPHY/Music; BIO032000 -
                   BIOGRAPHY & AUTOBIOGRAPHY / Social Activists; BIO022000
                   BIOGRAPHY & AUTOBIOGRAPHY / Women; MUS031000-MUSIC /
                   Genres & Styles / Rap & Hip-hop; MUSIC / Genres & Styles / Rhythm
                   & Blues see Genres & Styles / Soul & R 'n B; SOC028000 SOCIAL
                   SCIENCE / Women's Studies; SOC001000 SOCIAL SCIENCE /
                   Ethnic Studies / African American Studies.

Identifiers: ISBN – 13 – 9798776697081 (alk. Hardcover); 978-1-947704-32-9 (alk. color paper); 13: 978-1-947704-96-1 (alk. b/w KDP paper); 13: 9781947704992 (alk. color hardback w/dust cover); 13: 978-1-947704-16-9 (alk. b/w hardback w/dust cover) | ISBN – 978-1-947704-24-4 (digital).

Printed in the United States of America
First Edition: 12 11 10 9 8 7 6 5 4 3 2nd Edition 1-Reprint; 2020. All Rights Reserved.

For more information contact:
DonnaInk Publications, L.L.C.
www.donnaink.net | contact@donnainkpublications.com | www.facesofrapmothers.com

TABLE OF CONTENTS

FOREWORD
JEFFREY COLLINS

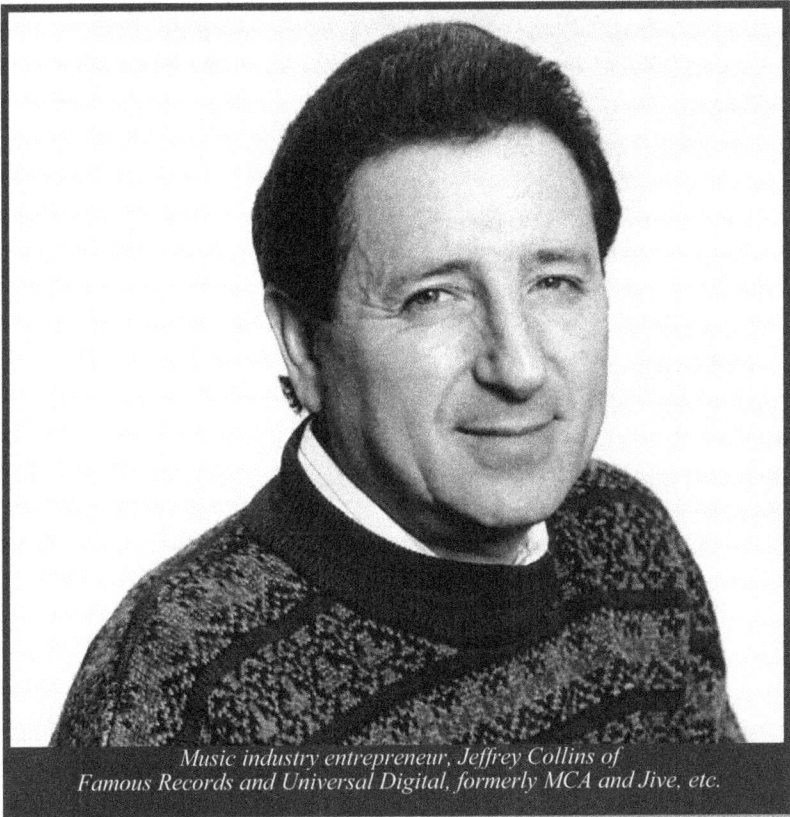

Music industry entrepreneur, Jeffrey Collins of Famous Records and Universal Digital, formerly MCA and Jive, etc.

PRIOR TO CANDICE BECOMING A RAP MOTHER (i.e.: a woman with a son who likes rap and hip-hop, and records rap songs), she was an advocate for civil rights. Her upbringing involved some of America's most revered civil and human rights activists, including Dr. Ophelia DeVore-Mitchell. Additionally, she had been involved in entertainment and media since her early youth. Her extended family have been entrenched in entertainment, which does not mean Candice was handed industry recognition because she earned her props at every stage of her business and career life.

As a mother, Candice has become a rap and hip-hop mom of two children, HONEY and KING THA RAPPER. She had the good fortune, as a teenager, to have friends extremely influential as rap and hip-hop artists – again – this did not predispose her children; instead, Candice's hard work educating them regarding entertainment and media while gaining access to commercials and programs at incredibly young ages, led to their path of discovery toward rap and hip-hop, which ultimately resulted in this public-cation.

Once her children were hooked on music, Candice began talking with mothers, sisters, aunts, cousins, and friends also involved in the rap and hip-hop medium – finally *Faces of Rap Mothers* platform was born and resulted in this book about mothers and their love for the children and the other stars in their lives who hail from rap and hip-hop origins. Of course, when fame results, love is conjoined with the natural enjoyment of success. And it should be. A mother's work is never done and the women in *Faces of Rap Mothers* are the very mothers who worked hard educating family members to shine in highly competitive markets.

When Candice agreed to permit her son, who calls himself, *KING THA RAPPER* to record rap music, *Rollin* was released through *Famous Records* and *Universal Digital* labels. *Rollin* had excellent reviews and rose in the charts significantly. Candice's daughter, Ricara Cheyenne aka *HONEY*, has also experienced hip-hop fandom with a promising future. With both a son, and daughter, in rap and hip-hop, comradery with other rap mothers was a logical outcome. Becoming increasingly affianced in rap and hip-hop – resulted in *Faces of Rap Mothers* platform and sharing rap experiences, which turned into a newly syndicated program alongside this first book in the *Faces of Rap Mothers* book series. Additionally, an upcoming children book series, *Rap Mothers Save The Day* features a first book release Valentine's Day 2020, titled, *Jay's First Day At A New School* and *Faces of Rap Mothers Fathers Editions* and *Presents Editions* are forthcoming.

Included in this compilation of contributory stories from women with family who are rap and hip-hop Superstars, are snippets of history from their myriad of collaborative mindsets, and old photos from rap moms, rap siblings, and/or the rappers themselves.

I feel certain these are going to be interesting series for readers and rap and hip-hop lovers.

About Jeffrey Collins: Mr. Collins heads *Universal Digital Distribution* and is a senior business consultant for several major artists and entertainment companies including, *Famous Music Group*.

Following stints running agencies and booking well-known acts such as *Dusty Springfield, Joe Cocker, Led Zeppelin, Lonnie Donegan, Moody Blues, The Beatles, etc. artisans* Collins represented also included soul singer *Donnie Elbert* and *Warren Davis Monday Band*. Jeffrey began a chain of retail record stores, and a wholesale distribution company, throughout the 70's and into the early 80's. He also began producing recording artists and developed *Echo Records* and *Vista Sounds* recording labels. He made reggae albums with releases from *Dennis Brown, Gregory Issacs, Johnny Clarke,* etc. with over one hundred (100) additional famous artists. His vocation brought more internationally known artists and producers from Europe, Jamaica, and the United States. In 1983, he setup an independent recording studio in Englewood, New Jersey and achieved great successes.

From this base, JC successfully worked with: *Adina Howard, Boogie Down Productions / KRS-ONE, Brenda K. Starr, Chill Rob G., Colon-El Abrams, Father MC, G-DEP, GRAVE-DIGGAZ, Positive K., Ram Squad, Ready For The World, Sunz Of Man, Wu-Tang Clan, and a host of other artists that obtained "major label recording deals"* with MCA, JIVE, KOCH, and others.

Although he could have retired at 50, when he moved with his family to Coral Springs, Florida, the call of music was still too loud to be ignored, and he decided in 2004 to enjoy the challenges within the recording industry once more and determined to keep doing what he knows and loves the best.

After first setting up a warehouse filled with vinyl records, Jeffrey became a consultant for a record pressing and CD plant, based in Plantation, Florida. He then started a new digital record label, *Famous Records, Corporation*, which releases and promotes music for artists worldwide via *Universal Digital Distribution*.

FAMOUS RECORDS / UNIVERSAL DIGITAL
Tel: 954-366-7419
Cell: 954-817-2878
Skype: jeffrey.echovista
www.UniversalDigitalDistribution.com

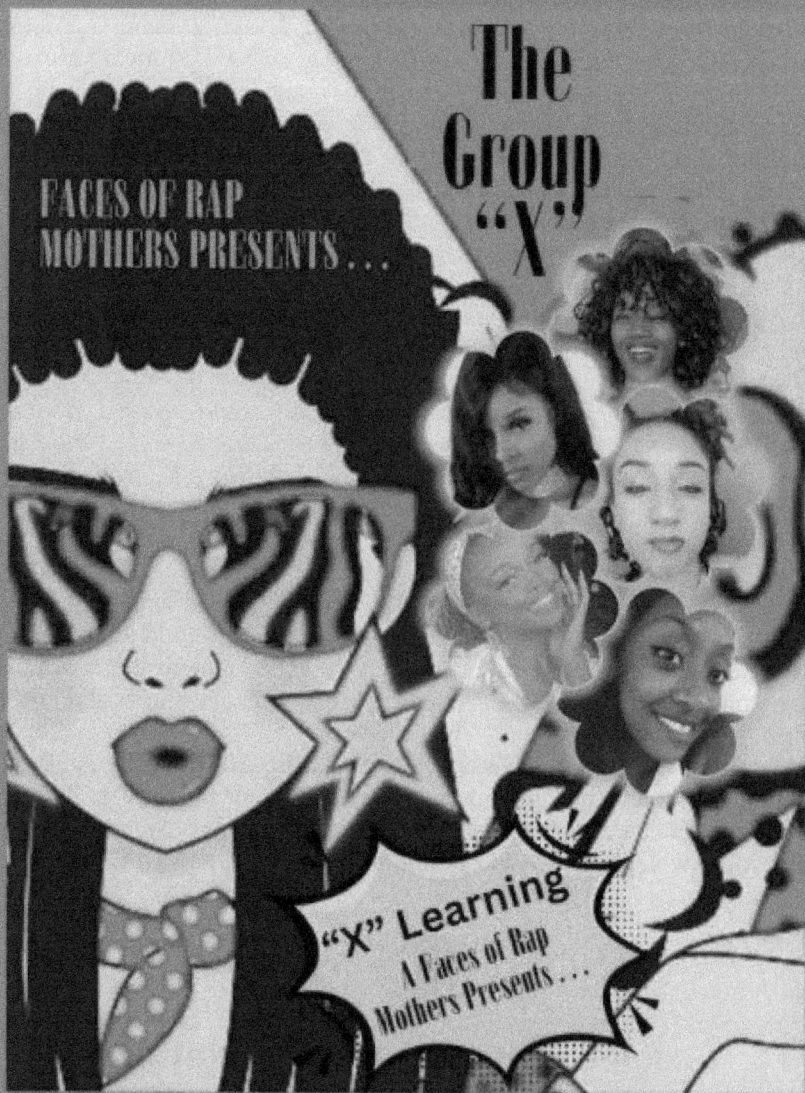

ACKNOWLEDGEMENTS
THANK YOU FOR YOUR SUPPORT

AT THIS TIME, I WANT TO TAKE a moment to acknowledge everyone who has helped bring this book to completion. First, and foremost, I want to thank God for his direction in moving me toward an abundant outlook throughout my life. He has aided me in all things I have set out to achieve and this has resulted in the triumphs *Faces of Rap Mothers* is experiencing.

My parents and my siblings, of course, aided me in the creation of this book, and the concept of these series titles, by giving me more drive and I am indebted to them for their support and love. Beyond this, my husband, who I love enormously, has upheld me every step of the way with this project, which was achieved in record time. Without my husband and children, these ideas, and this book, would not have been accomplished.

To the contributors of *Faces of Rap Mothers*, I want to applaud each wholeheartedly. We have evolved while experiencing profound outcomes in our own personal journeys alongside our families involved in the rap and hip-hop industry. We share a sameness in love and respect for the icons we relate to who live within the entertainment world. Moving through life with them, has been, and remains, an all-encompassing experience. We maintain strong synergies in our families that are vital to us all. As icons go, ups and downs associated with fame and its effects on its angels, include us and each of you as contributors to my book. Often, we remain silent in our life's purpose. As "Queens" living day-to-day – we reflect on our loved ones and their passions are directly attuned to our own.

Faces of Rap Mothers contributors know each of us are called upon to remain steadfast and *best represent home and hearth* for the Superstars we love. It goes without saying a major shout out, and acknowledgement to *Faces of Rap Mothers* contributors, is essential (listed alphabetically by last name):

- ➢ Honey Blunt
- ➢ Monica Davis
- ➢ Shonta Gibson (Queen G)
- ➢ Angela Guyton Gilchrist

> ➢ Tyaunna Harris

> ➢ Angela Hicks (O.G. LIL MAMA)

> ➢ Lena Moss

> ➢ Jamie Paris

> ➢ Nina Womack

> ➢ Sharon Lynette Young (Berreta)

Thank you, ladies, for contributing to this compilation. In addition to each of you, additional chapters recognize *Mrs. Shirley Curley, Godmother of Rap and Hip-hop*; *OG DUV MAC DOGG* a good friend of mine, and part of *Tha Snoop Dogg Experience*; and *Jamika Lawson Smith* the Minister for the *Faces of Rap Mothers* and *Rap Mothers Save the Day Series* books.

An important honorable mention is directed toward Mr. Jeffrey Collins who wrote the Foreword to *Faces of Rap Mothers*. Mr. Collins is a world-renown director, producer, publicist, record label owner, and sound engineer who extends well-over forty (40) years of music industry contributions. Thank you, for taking time to share thoughts, well wishes and understanding of *Faces of Rap Mothers*.

Also, a big thank you to my publisher, **DonnaInk Publications, L.L.C.** publishing house, Beat Deep Books and Little Buggy Productions Imprints. This small, woman-owned, traditional, and Indie publishing house features over thirty (30) eclectic authors and works for discriminating readers. Ms. Quesinberry is a truly professional ghostwriter with credit and the series merchandiser, publicist, and publisher for all the *Faces of Rap Mothers* books in each of the five series. Without Ms. Quesinberry's expertise, my book series would still be an idea. Donna, as I often say, *you are an angel – thank you*! You make my thoughts and words shine.

Ms. Quesinberry asked me to include Mr. Steven Kay, United Kingdom, who aided with the original integration of my book as another **DonnaInk Publications, L.L.C.** author, be recognized. Thank you, Steven Kay, for being gracious to collaborate with me while you were in LA.

The most important thanks go to readers, fans, and enthusiasts – without each of you – no book exists. We pray you ENJOY this book and the many more to come in the *Faces of Rap Mothers* and *Rap Mothers Save The Day Series*!

INTRODUCTION
FACES OF RAP MOTHERS

THE WORLD OF RAP AND HIP-HOP has historical origins relative to the bards. Nearly every culture has a form of the bards through their community of storytellers. While some people may view rap and hip-hop as rant / vent, or even sexual tirades set to deep beats; the reality is, every culture has used story and a driving beat to convey history and communal messages. To start our journey of back-stories and images – understanding the medium of rap and hip-hop's origins is the best place to begin.

Music, a meeting place of spoken word and story, delivered through emotional, intense, or sensual representations exudes the mythos and legends fables have conveyed to communities of listeners as observers who bent an ear, mind, and heart to receive messages. The fact intensity is driven in rap and hip-hop may have its very roots not only in hardships artists have endured, but also in generations of recorded words produced to lyrical format shared as shamanic messages with beautiful declarations. It is no surprise Maya Angelou observed, *I think a number of the leaders are, whether you like it or not, in the hip-hop generation. And when they understand enough, they will do wonders. I count on them.* Acknowledgments of life, and its wisdoms, shared through story, beats, and lyrics unites humanity breaking barriers otherwise unavailable.

Within rap and hip-hop mindsets, hard-hitting lyrical spits result in enhanced awareness of the human condition. Women contributors to this first edition of the *Faces of Rap Mothers* series, are acutely aware of the stature fans, and aficionados, hold when reflecting on the artisans they often mirror. Lifestyles of rap and hip-hop icons are disclosed in *Faces of Rap Mothers* and share the reality rap and hip-hop icons are, in fact, often upwardly mobile achievers. The Superstars' children attend gifted and talented programs. They are engaged in musical studies, acting classes and work toward another generation of success. They are not handed golden gloves. Talent takes dedication. However, readers and fans, gain awareness of rap and hip-hop roots in this book and these are a far greater service than any representative façades.

Beyond the physical origins of rap and hip-hop, are linear patterns of music production and development with roots in the Caribbean and West Africa when referencing rap and hip-hop – so say the scholars. Of course, South American, Middle Eastern, and Indian cultural influences resonant rap and hip-hop as performance arts. There are elements of European folk music every now and again. The soul of rap and hip-hop is solely an American treasure. Founded in, and around, America's urban and inner-city experiences, where street performers and underground movements hold solid resonance, the truth of rap and hip-hop is proclaimed.

Caribbean storytellers use rhymes to share tales, and West African griots shared stories gaining structure through drumbeats, but in the Americas First Nation shaman shared stories to drums, South Americans added flutes and instrumentals and the movement has been epic ever since. The official origins of rap and hip-hop are slated to be derived from the 70's where DJs began recording loops with New York City being the jumping off point. Post-*Woodstock, Vietnam, John F. Kennedy, Robert Kennedy,* and *Martin Luther King* jarring events, artists' minds have reminisced while regarding civil rights and the unfortunate suites of riots and hoped for outcomes . . . Rap and hip-hop's true origins started well-before the 70's during the 50's and 60's where Black musicians took the industry by storm after weathered storm demonstrating implausible successes the 20's, 30's, and 40's wouldn't permit. Albeit the blues, jazz and gritty *Dirty South* beginnings were resolute in those eras. Life, and art, has its way.

The 70's provided amplification in rap and hip-hop when musical inno-vations and social influence benchmarked its creative journey. The history of story, and folklore, introduced to industrial engines resulted in a gener-ation of sound ignited with electronics, experimental synergizing sounds, and videography as the most well-recognized music of the 20th century. A gardenbed of new and innovative lyricists, and performance and slam poets, delivered an artful community that has marched ever onward since.

In the 80's, the Nation was ripe for the Golden Era of rap and hip-hop, which exploded across America - moving from New York City - winding up in California where *West Coast* resides. As a result, a clash among performers opened the flood gates for women who had a tendency 'not' to fight and to keep their eyes on the ball with a focus on success. *It takes a woman, right?* This vision of women lends great triumphs when shared in a compilation such as this where the contributors in this title underscore the reality women are wisest.

Knowing the past – is half the battle toward a better future - and the newest generation of performance artists in this genre appreciate the needle drops of the 70's and 80's and couple those with lyrics speaking toward a greater good while embracing epic stories, folklore, and some raunchy realities that make rap and hip-hop what it is today.

The *Faces of Rap Mothers* continues the rap and hip-hop journey by providing fans a backdrop of realism associated with the industry's icons. contributors of *Faces of Rap Mothers* are associated with these Superstars and their predecessors from the 50's and 60's – and they are leading those breaking new beats today. Candy, and her contributors, know the intimate details in the evolution of the deep beats, intensity, stories, and imagery shared in rap and hip-hop because they live them in every conceptual paradigm a human being can.

Faces of Rap Mothers takes readers behind the scenes and provides "little known" and "virtually unknown" facts of interest with unwitting asides. Knowing there is more than meets the eye, no matter the genre, is exciting; and, more importantly, *Faces of Rap Mothers* entertains readers, fans, and devotees hence the creation of these stories.

This is the first volume of the *Faces of Rap Mothers* series. Each volume is intended to feature unique contributors, their backstories, and elaborations of prior contributor stories as well. Some crossover and repeats may exist from book to book starting out – eventually all new rap mothers are contributors for each new title release.

FACES OF RAP MOTHERS MUSIC GROUP

rap, hip hop & funk

www.facesofrapmothers.com

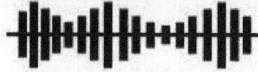

FACES OF RAP MOTHERS

TELEVISION NETWORK

DEDICATION
MRS. SHIRLEY CURLEY

I**N DEVELOPING THIS TITLE**, as the original volume / edition of *Faces of Rap Mothers,* I want to identify Mrs. Shirley Curley as the *Den Mother of Rap and Hip-hop*. Mrs. Curley is the Queen of the *West Coast* and *Dirty South*; she is the *Ultimate Queen of all Rap Mothers*.

Shirley, born in Louisiana, traveled throughout the world – Hollywood's greatest rap and hip-hop entertainers refer to her as mom, including over one hundred and fifty (150) creative artists derived from historical annals as well as up-n-coming artisans.

Mrs. Curley taught youth she encountered to be the best they could in life. She was voted most loving mother in *West Coast* hip-hop and is recognized for being an amazing woman who gave birth to more multi-million-dollar award-winning children (with four [4] successful sons) than any other rap and hip-hop mother in history. She is definitively blessed with an abundance of excellence, noting the successes her sons have attained - due to Shirley's parentage.

Her eldest son, *TJ Pops Johnson*, is *Candy Strother DeVore-Mitchell's* (my) Godbrother. He is also father of the *West Coast Grammy* awarded *Superstar Slim Da Mobster*. As Shirley's oldest son, *TJ Pops Johnson* is also Godfather to Candy's (my) children – one of whom is *Universal Recording* artist, *KING THA RAPPER*.

Mrs. Curley also gave birth to twins who are equally amazing characters. Pastor Ronald Johnson has a church in Dallas Texas. He is a kind, loving soul, with a Godly spirit. Through his ministry, he has touched many lives. Shirley's other twin son, Donald Johnson, Candy is proud to call her Godbrother and admits she loves him with all her heart – words just cannot explain. He is a great man.

Donald's son is a *West Coast* hip-hop artist signed *to Warner Brothers* records. Donald, during the multi-million-dollar deal of *Dr. Dre*, served as the brains of the matter.

Shirley's youngest son *Mario "Chocolate" Johnson*, has incredible stats as a producer of award-winning rap and hip-hop artists, such as *Dr. Dre, Eminem, Havoc the Mouthpiece, Snoop Dogg, The Alcoholics, Vanilla Ice, Xibit*, etc. *Chocolate's* stats are extraordinary, and he is gifted as a musical genius. At age sixteen (16), *Chocolate* produced the Grammy award hit song, *Ice Ice Baby*. It grossed over five-million dollars in sales and *Chocolate* produced this award-winning title in Mrs. Shirley Curley's garage in Dallas, Texas.

We, in the rap and hip-hop community, are happy Shirley Curley blessed the world with her amazing children and grandchildren, through her multi-million-dollar, award-winning, DNA.

The greatest element of Mrs. Curley's legacy involves the fact she trained her children, and all God's children she connected with, to spread love as much as humanly possible by preaching God's word like her son Pastor Ronald Johnson or in any fashion possible. Shirley believes love is the best measure of the human spirit. All her children spread love through preaching and teaching. Each of her sons are involved in creative arts, such as engineering, producing and writing.

As the *Queen Den Mother of Faces of Rap Mothers*, Shirley Curley remains a highly respected *West Coast* and *Dirty South* icon where some Hollywood's greatest view her as a wise educator with words of positive healing and love . . . a quote from Mrs. Curley, the *Ultimate Queen Rap and Hip-Hop Den Mothers*:

> *"Let noting come before your children. Love your children. It's not about the material things in life, such as Jordan's; instead, what is important is for your children to know they are truly loved."*

Shirley Curley, this book is dedicated to you, we thank you for all you have accomplished as a Queen involved not only in rap and hip-hop, but also in our lives.

Mrs. Shirley Curley – looking fine in the day.

Mrs. Shirley Curley's 75th Birthday Celebration with her four sons.

FACES OF
RAP MOTHERS

PROLOGUE
ABOUT THIS BOOK

FOR STARTERS, SOME CHAPTERS FEATURE more background development than others. Many are photographic renderings where the image and visual discernment is the reader's takeaway – mapping their own interpretations. Like all art, photographs are open to the eye of the observer. "Some" of the images included in *Faces of Rap Mothers*, are old and worn – these are not industry images by professional photographers at red carpet events; there are "those images" because they matter; however, most images included are from home events with family and friends or at extended family and friends' homes. And, back in the day, let us face it, photos were shot from disposable cameras and had to be developed at the department store or the infamous polaroid was deployed for instant viewing. The cool aspect of this is, as readers, you are enabled to join in on homespun memories previously undisclosed to media.

Due to the nature of images shared, we were unable to reproduce and/or regenerate them in a modern lens . . . so we ask readers to not be judgmental regarding these photographs. It is the hope of the *Faces of Rap Mothers* each of you enjoy the "moments" in the life of . . . their extended family and friends . . . many of whom are among America's rich and famous. Use an eye fashioned to your own *home stash of old photos* everyone adores and wishes could be rendered in modernity while knowing it is what it is. Also, please note, many images say "friend" or "celebrities" due to the fact though rich and famous – without verification of the people in an image – they could not be listed but you will recognize who the folks are with ease, and we apologize for any inconvenience this conveys to you as a reader. We worked to produce this title in record time and should have all "names" in the next volumes.

Future volumes in the *Faces of Rap Mothers* series will include additional rap and hip-hop women contributors with images and backstories not included in this edition; included in Book Two are Carlene Corsey (academy award nominee) and others.

A little more about the book's development – the divider fleuron is an image of a record with a flame and the word hip-hop on it . . . when you see this, if you are not aware of why it is included, it is where the structure of the read moves elementally to another phase "or" a natural "significant" pause occurs moving readers to a new thought sequence. Plus, it is cool to look at, and thankfully, a Creative Commons - a happy to glad in book production.

This title is available in soft cover black and white (b/w) and in soft cover color. It is also available in hardcover black and white (b/w) and in hardcover color. An e-Edition "may" become available soon. Signature copies will be made available for an extra $10.00 to $20.00 per copy regardless of print style. Any/all signed copies ship on unique timelines to secure signatures.

When able, names throughout the title are listed alphabetically by last name or by group name where a last name is not identified. This is to eliminate any confusion regarding Who's Who placements. Also, not every contributor is a "mother" of a rap and/or hip-hop artist; however, each are "mothers" involved within the rap and hip-hop industry who provide appropriate guidance toward their children and others' children.

The creators of this title are developing the *Rap Mothers Save The Day, Jay's First Day At A New School* for a Valentine's Day release and also *Faces of Rap Mothers Fathers Editions* and *Faces of Rap Mothers Presents* . . . *Group X* for the "first" presentation, with the Curvy Queens of Dallas in the "second" presentation, and Bonnie Williams (Stanley "Tookie" Williams wife) in the "third" presentation. *Faces of Rap Mothers* contributors, and Candy Strother DeVore-Mitchell, extend sincere thanks for reader interest.

Now, let us move into Book One of the *Faces of Rap Mothers*, which has been created to entertain, educate, and share what is now, American folklore, and the world rap and hip-hop represents.

EPIGRAPH
MAYA ANGELOU

I *THINK A NUMBER OF* the leaders are,
whether you like it or not,
in the hip-hop generation.

And when they understand enough,
they'll do wonders. I count on them.

CHAPTER ONE
CANDY STROTHER DEVORE MITCHELL

Candy Strother DeVore Mitchell.

BORN IN JAMAICA QUEENS New York, Candy was raised primarily by her mother *Blanche Abrams DeVore-Mitchell*, and her grandmother, *Blanche DeVore*. They resided in a large home in Queens. Much of their family was always present. There were many aunts and uncles and, of course, plenty of cousins as well.

One of Candy's aunts was a celebrity, and civil rights hero, who worked alongside *Dr. Martin Luther King* to fight for our country and civil rights. Candy's Auntie Ophelia DeVore-Mitchell or Auntie O, as she was referred to, provides a vivid memory for Candy. Auntie O was consistently around the home where Candy was raised as Candy's grandmother's sister.

Dr. Ophelia DeVore-Mitchell was born 12 August 1922 and passed away 28 February 2014. She was an American businesswoman, model, and publisher; also, the first model of African American descent in the United States and in 1946, established *The Grace Del Marco Agency* - the first modeling agency in America for people of color. The agency's startup took place in Candy's grandmother, Blanche DeVore's home. Business was conducted in the basement and Superstars such as *Diane Carroll, Helen Reddy*, and *Cecily Tyson* frequented there. People with amazing talent began to gain career recognition through Auntie O's agency; Candy was raised in earshot of it all.

Best wishes to Ophelia De Vore

Jimmy Carter

Dr. Emma Ophelia DeVore-Mitchell, Candy's Auntie O.

Dr. Emma Ophelia DeVore-Mitchell, born in Edgefield, South Carolina, was one ten (10) children born to John Walter DeVore and Mary Emma Strother. Her ancestry is African American, German American, and Native American (Cherokee). Her father owned a road contracting business, and her mother was an educator and musician. Her father mentored Emma in communicating with people and her mother stressed proper appearance, education, and etiquette. She attended segregated schools until she was nine (9) years of age; then she moved to Winston-Salem to live with her mother's brother. When she finally moved to New York City, she lived with Candy's family. Eventually, Ophelia graduated from *Hunter College High School* and went on to *New York University* to major in mathematics and minor in languages. In 1941, she married Harold Carter who worked as a firefighter while she studied advertising, fashion, and public relations – they had five (5) children together. Later, she married Vernon Mitchell. Auntie O was featured in Brian Lanker's *I Dream a World*, collection of portraits and biographies of Black women who helped change

America. She was honored by the *Fashion Institute of Technology* and the *Fashion Arts Xchange, Inc.* for contributions to entertainment and fashion.

As CEO, and publisher, of *The Columbus Times* newspaper in Columbus, Georgia – Ophelia ran one of the first Black newspapers until her retirement in 2009. Currently, one of Auntie O's other granddaughters manages the paper after she passed in 2014.

Being raised with a continuously powerful influence at home, *Candy Strother DeVore-Mitchell's* joining in the evolution of the advancement of colored people (as referenced) was, of course, a natural one. Human rights were daily conversations throughout Candy's life along with entertainment, fashion, and media. It would be a surprise "if" Candy were not involved in civil rights, entertainment, and media. All the above gained her attention as she shares on pages that follow . . .

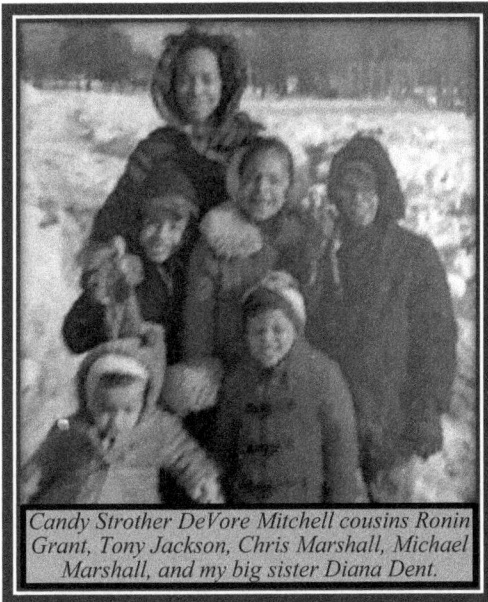

Candy Strother DeVore Mitchell cousins Ronin Grant, Tony Jackson, Chris Marshall, Michael Marshall, and my big sister Diana Dent.

As a budding young person, I was greatly influenced by my Auntie O. Her knowledge intrigued me. Our family was huge, like our home, and I grew up feeling a lot of love due to this. My sisters, brothers, stepsisters, stepbrothers, cousins and informally adopted siblings were all welcome in our home; this included aunts and uncles, etc. While I grew up, I played with my sister Angelina Mann, my cousins Mark Jackson and Maria Marshall, and my big sister Diana.

We were all very close.

Candy's Godsister
Candice Outlaw & son Shymel.

In addition, I had Godsisters, Candice Outlaw (named after me and Shantell) and Towana and Jauda who always played with us. Thank God, my grandmother *Blanche DeVore's* home was bountiful. My Godsisters, Candice and Shantell, were *Superstar Tupac Shakur's* cousins and grew up in *Tupac's* home.

For a while, I went to live with my father and had an opportunity to spend time with my brother, *Superstar Producer, Guy Mitchell*. As a platinum and gold record producer, my brother produced *Bobby Brown, Peabo Bryson, Mariah Carey, Alisha Keys, The Commodores, The Deuce, TLC, Usher,* etc. He influenced my interest in creative arts and music.

Later, when I was sixteen (16), I moved to Hollywood and began acting, modeling, and working with filmmaking. *The Jackson Family* and I met. We mingled with the Rockefeller's and hung out with the owner of the Lakers. When in the Hollywood area, I lived in Bel Air and attended parties at *Aaron Spellings'* home in Hollywood Hills. Sye Winthrop, owner of *Columbia Pictures*, Nina Womack, and I were regulars at *Hugh Hefner's Playboy Mansion* parties. I had the opportunity to hang out with *Arsenio Hall, Eddie Murphy* and *Prince* and must admit we shared amazing teenage years among our friends, and in our family.

Candy's brother
Guy Mitchell.

My big sister, Diana became a *Marvelette* for a brief period. Our Godmother, *Glady's Horton* had to replace a member of the group on tour because a member of the original group was deceased. She graciously hired my sister to go on tour and perform with her for a short time. I remember my sister practicing *Please, Mr. Postman*, and all the other great songs *Gladys Horton & the Marvelettes* performed. My big sister had a blast being a *Marvellete* for the short period of time our Godmother hired her. Our family still has the videos of their live performances. For a while, my beautiful intelligent, talented, and loving sister, who

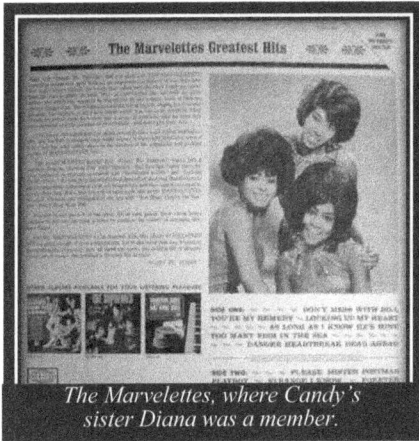

The Marvelettes, where Candy's sister Diana was a member.

I love more than life itself, Diana Dent Mitchell, was the youngest member of the Motown group, *The Marvelettes*.

Entertainment has remained about my family my entire life, since I lived in my grandmother's home. *Della Fitzgerald* came to our home whenever she was in New York.

She, and niece Janis, would stay at grandmother's home in Baisley Park in Queens.

Again in Hollywood; I met and hung out with *Faces of Rap Mothers*, *Berreta* (Sharon Lynette Young), *Monica Davis,* and *Nina Womack* – we were friends with *Bobby Brown, Natalie Cole, Ice Cube, Chuck D of Public Enemy, Dr. Dre, Sheila-E, Eazy-E, Arsenio Hall, Whitney Houston, Suge Knight, Eddie Murphy and his family, Salt-N-Pepa, Prince, Hank Shocklee, Will Smith, The Jackson Family, The Wayan Bros., Vanity, Stevie Wonder*, etc. It was an endless list, these are some of the easiest to recollect – my most memorable experiences were with *Prince, The Jackson Family* and *Stevie Wonder*.

Of course, later in life, spending time with *Whitney Houston* was a lot of fun. I genuinely loved Bobby and Whitney and their daughter. When they were together at a gathering, there was magic in the air. They were truly in love, the type of love you feel when you are in the room with people in love. You could tell Whitney and Bobby were together – no matter what tabloids say.

Not long after that, I began to have my own family and children, so I started my own company, *DeVore Entertainment*, which became *Black Cash Universal Studios Entertainment*. Originally, the latter was to manage my children, but with immediate success – it blossomed into more.

HONEY began modeling and winning beauty pageants; she received the title of *Lil Miss Los Angeles in 2002*. My children were invited to appear as guests on the *Jenny Jones Show*. We attended, and the ratings were so high, the producer wanted the us to return and film another episode right away; so, we flew back to Chicago to film another segment as requested.

Jenny Jones Show, where two of Candy's children were featured as guests in the child pageant participant's segment.

Rico, my son, landed film roles with *Jessica Alba, ATT, Nick Cannon, Samuel Jackson, Sprint,* and many others. My son, United States Army Officer Lawrence Lee, modeled and was featured on billboards in every city across the United States. His work included *Chevrolet Malibu* and *Kmart* advertisements, magazines, and with pop star *Thalia* and *Superstar Mogul, Martha Stewart*. Yet another of my sons, *Universal Recording Artist KING THA RAPPER* was my Taco Bell baby. He was aired in his first commercial at three (3) months of age, where he was cast as a newborn in a nursery.

Tyler Lee, another of my sons, just returned from Spain where he received training for the 2020 Junior Olympics in soccer, he is fourteen (14) years of age and I have faith he is going to succeed.

Following the positive examples my Auntie O represented as a *Hollywood Agent to the Stars* – taught me to listen to the world around me and to find success for my children. Of course, for every gain in life, there is negative opposition and in the process of managing my children's careers, I became a victim of lies and government fraud. Children's Services determined I wanted to human traffic my children and I had to

Candy's son US Army Ofc. Lawrence Lee.

6

battle the courts and fight for my children's and my rights. After being falsely accused, and a victim of family court, I learned the child custody system is a dilemma plaguing many American lives at this time. I learned trafficking of children also occurs through the court system.

After discovering more, and self-educating, I began to advocate to aid families who need support while in the cruxes of family court fraud. Nearing a billion dollar a year business, family court is extremely hard on targeted families who are often minority and/or single. Children are wrongfully removed from families whenever, and wherever, possible. Localities earn approximately $250,000 per child if they can be absconded into foster care from their families. It is not about right and wrong any longer – it is about demographics and who can be victimized with the least issue. Americans do not realize how much revenue child custody and family court are making for the court system and communities where cases are heard. Each case in court regarding custody, earns the court between $8K and $15K a month throughout the duration of the litigation, for instance and people are generally unaware of this statistic.

Candy Strother DeVore Mitchell with Gilbert Jalapeno representing families and their children suffering Family Court injustice at an Affiliated Peoples Alliance Campaign such as Black and Brown Makes Gold.

On top of that, each parent must hire an attorney who average per custodial litigant between $80K and $250K – many parents pay as high as $500K before their case is complete. Then, support industries involved in document production, printing, hotels, experts, psychologists, etc. are also earning and it has become big business on the backs of children and families. If you just use some basic math and multiply the average costs of the hundreds of family court cases per year in counties across America, it is easy to understand real child trafficking is wielded under the guise of law acting in a child's best interest. It is a despot system of injustice and I fell victim to it as did my children. Once done, you cannot recover the loss of the act of child custody and fraud wielded upon families such as my own.

Just counting 100 families with the statistics I have listed here results in $71M a year in earnings for a locality. Now, who is child trafficking?

In meeting other families with wrongfully removed children – I have learned a lot about this broken system of justice. It was created to help families and is being used to hurt them. I know my own mother, grandmother and Aunt, *Dr. Ophelia DeVore-Mitchell* who aided *Dr. Martin*

Trayvon Williams and Gilbert Jalapeno – fighting family court injustice through the Black and Brown Makes Gold Campaign that APA represented.

Luther King and all Americans who become aware of the abuse in family court, would expect me, or one another once knowledgeable, to take the mantle to fight for the rights of children and families.

During my case, and since that time, I have joined forces with Gilbert Jalapeño, the Founder of the *Affiliated People's Alliance (APA)*. We have a human rights campaign through his 501(c)3 that thwarts family court injustice. The most popular campaign I have been involved with, through APA, was the *Black and Brown Makes Gold Campaign* featuring five (5) time *Nobel Peace Prize Nominee, Stanley Tookie Williams'* son, Trayvon Williams. Both Gilbert Jalapeño and I started the campaign titled, *Black and Brown Makes Gold*. For my part, I was on the news in California and at court houses holding picket signs frequently as an activist to fight for rights of children and families; also, to stop human trafficking in and out of the government system. My friend, Gilbert Jalapeno, is releasing his own book and story titled, *From Spicy 2 Sweet*, which promises to be an informative release regarding the family court system and people it denigrates – I look forward to the potential of reading it.

Around this time, my son, *KING THA RAPPER* began getting interested in rap and hip-hop. He had a lot of experience in front of television cameras since birth and had been in recording studios at *Universal City* since the age five (5) thanks to his Godmother Julie Clark who is as close to me as my own sister. KING asked me to help him with his music, and we expanded the family entertainment company to not only manage actors, dancers, and models, but also to include musicians, producers, rappers, and singers.

KING THA RAPPER and Black Ca$h Records.

KING THA RAPPER met Jeffrey Collins, CEO of *Famous Records* and *Universal Digital* and the rest is history. JC formerly ran *MCA* and *Jive*. He knew KING was gifted having produced child musicians previously. *KING THA RAPPER* released his first record at age thirteen (13) with a record deal. KING writes, produces, arranges, and engineers his own music and taught himself to play piano, saxophone, and bass guitar. He did attend a *Los Angeles County Academy* for gifted children and was thirty-seven (37) nationwide on hip-hop charts for five (5) months in a row with his hit song, *I.M.O.* (*In My Opinion*). The single includes *West Coast* legend, *KURUPT* of *Tha Dogg Pound* and *Young Gotti*.

KING THA RAPPER also recorded, *Popular* with *West Coast* hip-hop artist *Timbo* and their single made it to #1 hip-hop charts on *Power 106-DJ Kiss* radio. Another of his singles was #6 on the hip-hop charts and included *Indica Walker*, Berreta's daughter who is an amazing vocalist. *Indica* and *KING THA RAPPER's* hit song titled, *So Far, So Close (feat. Indica Walker)* - was very well received.

As *Black Cash Universal Studio Entertainment* grew, I had the shock of my life, nearly dying from cancer. My body was riddled with the miserable disease, I was in a coma for three weeks and hospitalized. Three of my major organs were removed. Thankfully, God brought me thru – I have a lot of unfinished business to attend to – it just isn't time for me to go. In my heart of hearts, I want to help all God's children - I believe I am here to love and help people and plan to use the remainder of my life in every conceivable way to aid people, including children and, of course, with emphasis on my own. Today, I continue to manage *Black Cash*

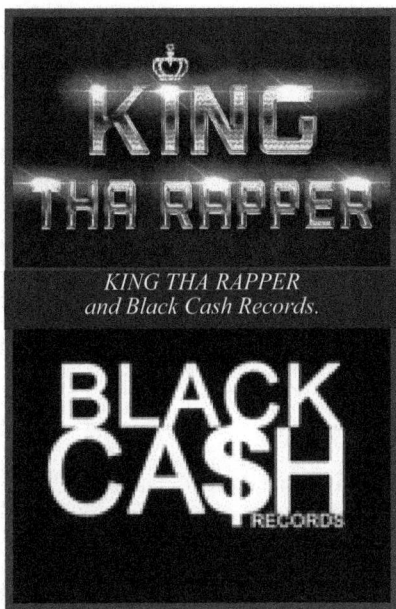

Universal Studio Entertainment and work, live, and love our Heavenly Father as do all the ladies from *Faces of Rap Mothers*.

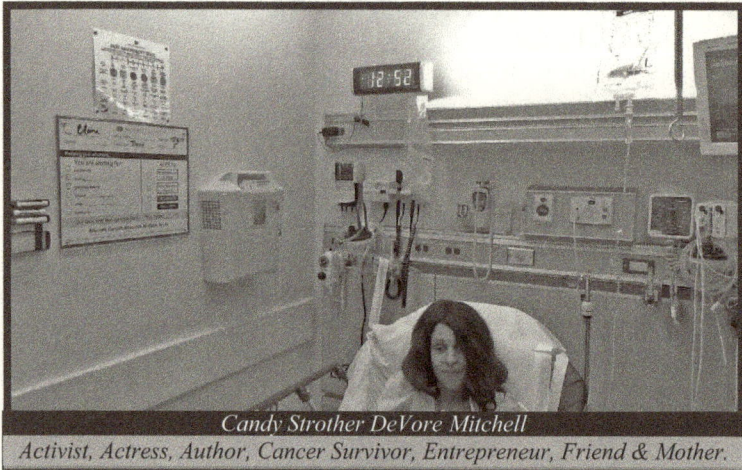

Candy Strother DeVore Mitchell
Activist, Actress, Author, Cancer Survivor, Entrepreneur, Friend & Mother.

Candy Strother DeVore Mitchell and Family
Chillin' at home

My children *HONEY* (with blonde hair) and *KING THA RAPPER* are both featured in a magazine with *Snoop Dogg* and *KURUPT* of *Tha Dogg Pound*, which is shared in the images that follow.

Left to right: Bobby Dragenit, OG DUV MAC, Honey, Snoop Dogg, Berreta, Candice Strother DeVore Mitchell & Richard.

11

My children remind me of my youth, and I must admit, living in sunny California and visiting the Palms Springs scene grew on me throughout our lives. Before I had my own family, my mother decided to help me with my dreams of following in Auntie O's footsteps. Three (3) days after I arrived in California, my mother signed me to an agent, and only one week later, I was cast as a model in *The Jackson Family's* music video. I was immediately in love with filming, cameras, and entertainment. My mother's foresight brought back all the excitement I felt around Auntie O at my grandmother's home.

KING THA RAPPER'S Grandmother – Margie Lee.

I began filming small roles in many different music videos and many small parts with fellow *Rap Mother Berreta*. While we were young, I took vocal performance lessons at *Paramount Pictures*, which was paid for by *Solar Records*. *Suge Knight's* brother *Wes Crocket*, owner of *Wes World Productions*, *Nina Womack* and I met *Snoop Dogg* and *Warren G* at age nineteen (19). We were all filming a music video in downtown Los Angeles. Each of us were striving to become celebrities – we all had small roles in *Lady of Rage* music video. At that time, *Snoop Dogg* was not famous, both Nina and I were shocked to learn *Snoop* and *Warren G* lived in the apartments located next door to ours with our home girl, Darvina who was pregnant with *Suge Knight's* son at the time. When *Warren G* and *Snoop Dogg* realized Nina lived in the building next door, they began to visit daily after work.

Back then, Warren and Snoop worked in the studio with *Dr. Dre*, *Warren G's* brother. Snoop was recording his first album, *Chronic* with *Dr. Dre*. It later became the album of the year and when it did – my next-door neighbor, and friend I loved, became a world-famous Superstar overnight. *Faces of Rap Mothers* star *Berreta* visited with Nina and I every day and she became Snoop and Warren's partner in spades. They played that card game eternally - Snoop declared it his favorite card game. Berreta, related to one of the most infamous backup singers in the world, *Val Young*, remained extremely close to Snoop over the years. The group of us lived on Whitley Avenue on the corner of Hollywood Boulevard. Our good friend eventually became the most infamous rapper in the world and, I must admit, it is cool to know him personally as a friend "first." He remains a good friend to all of us, regardless of his level of success, and that is a real person.

Around this same time, I was influenced by my Godmother *Gladys Horton* – who was lead singer of *Motown's Marvelettes*. I lived with her from age sixteen (16) to nineteen (19) and she sparked my interest in entertainment, watching her and *The Marvelettes* rehearse and perform shows for the *Motown Revue*, etc.

As they say, the rest was history, and is more easily conveyed in photographs shared on the pages that follow. I want to mention a few additional things before the photos prevail. The first is, I am thankful you have taken the time to purchase this, Book One of the *Faces of Rap Mothers*. We are already working on Book Two and developing the children's book to promote positivity and good in life for children.

In closing my chapter, it saddens me to share *Faces of Rap Mothers Jamie Paris* passed suddenly on 27 September 2019. While this book initially went to press week of the 27th – Jamie was not able to "see" it. A more appropriate tribute will be shared in future Books of *Faces of Rap Mothers*. Today, I want to share, everyone who knew Jamie Paris knows how stellar a human being she was. She shared light and love in all ways. It hurts she has moved on to the next chapter of existence, away from us. We are thankful to have held opportunity to refer to Jamie as our friend.

She shared a truly abundant mindset that remains uplifting and was never overstated or under-representative of any fellow rap mothers. I want to raise a prayer and applaud my dear friend *Jamie Paris* as a *Faces of Rap Mothers Queen.* Rest easy *Queen Jamie Paris* - while keeping an eye on us from heaven. We love you.

Jamie Paris doing what she loved best in life – being maternal.

JP Cali Smoov's father, Stevie Debarge.

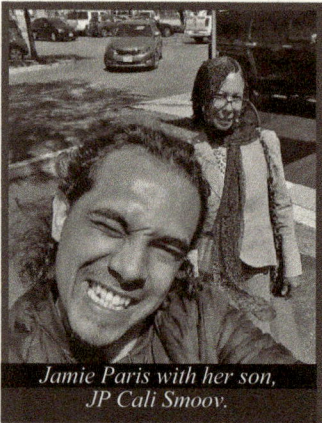

Jamie Paris with her son, JP Cali Smoov.

Jamie Paris and her son.

From left to right: Candy's son, Lawrence Lee,
Whitney Houston, Candy Strother DeVore Mitchell and Bobby Kristina.

House party with Candy's son, Lawrence Lee, Bobby Kristina,
Candy Strother DeVore Mitchell and others.

KING THA RAPPER & KURUPT's IMO hit single & in image below. pictured with Lawrence Lee and Candy Strother DeVore Mitchell.

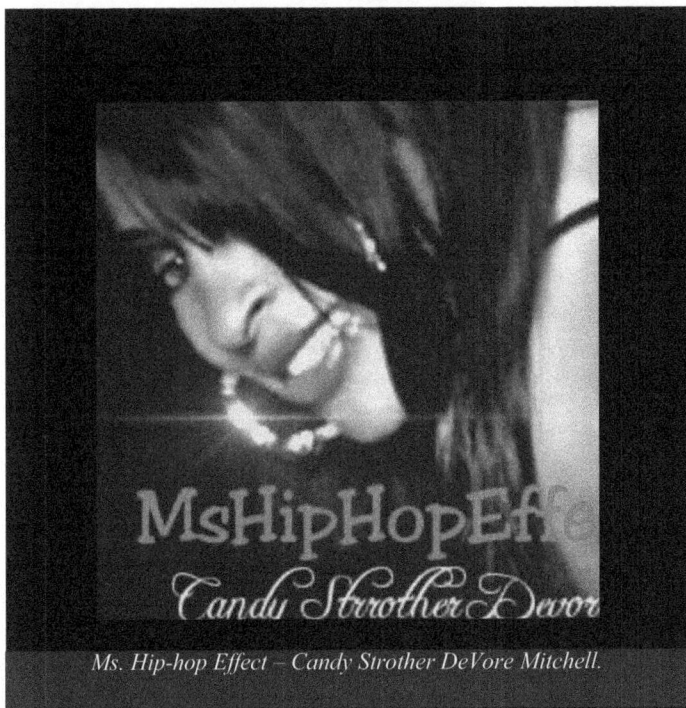

Ms. Hip-hop Effect – Candy Strother DeVore Mitchell.

Snoop Dogg, OG DUV MAC DOGG, and
Candy Strother DeVore Mitchell.

United States Army Officer Lawrence Lee with
Candy Strother DeVore Mitchell, his momma.

18

OG LIL MAMA and Candy Strother DeVore Mitchell.

At Snoop Dogg's book signing for, From Crook to Cook at B&N.

Candy Strother DeVore Mitchell with Bobby Brown's twin nephews up & coming up rappers Jerod & Herod Brown. Superstar Bobby Brown's nephews have had multiple interviews on the Nancy Grace Show and the Dr. Drew Show.

Original Dogg Pound member, OG DUV MAC DOGG with business partner Candy & Pete Sake of APA Human Rights 501(c)3 – filming a campaign for Gilbert Jalapeno's APA Organization to Stop Human Trafficking of Children.

19

Candy's cellphone capture of her beautiful baby sister, Ashley Mitchell & her friend.

Cousin Karlton Jones jazz musician & producer nominated for a Grammy on stage with Gerald Albright.

Goddaughters West Coast Girl's Music Group, JCM and their mother, Geneava Bryant, performing for the community per request of the Mayor of Compton.

Candy at an event as an activist for the rights of children and their families – against unfair kidnap and exploitation of children as well as child trafficking of children through the guise of the legal system.

The Presidential Inaugural Committee

requests the honor of your presence

to participate in the

inauguration of

Barack H. Obama

as President of the United States of America

and

Joseph R. Biden, Jr.

as Vice President of the United States of America

on Monday, the twenty-first of January

two thousand and thirteen

in the city of Washington

Candy's eldest son, Ricardo Strother DeVore, was invited to the United States White House for the work he performed for disadvantaged youth. President Barack Obama and Vice President Joe Biden extended a sincere vote of thanks for the honor extended to Candy's son Ricardo.

Candy's sister Diana with Ambassador Andrew Young who is a longtime friend of her family. Ambassador Young also with Dr. Ophelia DeVore Mitchell, famous civil and human rights activist.

Candy Strother DeVore Mitchell's son, Tyler awarded for martial arts efforts.

Candy with KING, Nina Womack, Tina Brown, and HONEY.

Candy with family and friends at LA event.

HONEY, Candy, Tina, Nina Womack, KING THA RAPPER and lil man.

Candy's Grandmother.

Candy's Auntie O
Dr. Ophelia DeVore-Mitchell.

Rico DeVore & Blair Underwood.

KING THA RAPPER & Rico DeVore.

Rico DeVore on Let's Be Whole.

US Army Lawrence Lee.

Jamie Paris & Candy Strother DeVore Mitchell at Arsenio's

Faces of Rap Mothers Show with
HONEY, Bonnie Williams, Candy & OG Lil Mama.

Candy with Mrs. Shirley Curley's eldest son, also her children's Godfather and her Godbrother, CEO of Poppas Kitchen Empire, Mr. TJ Pops Johnson.

Slim the Mobster (Anthony Johnson), Superstar Rapper TJ Pops Johnson's son who wrote and produced a hit song along with Dr. Dre. Slim is a Godbrother to KING THA RAPPER & Honey as well as all of Candy's children.

APA Event.

Candy's son Ricardo on the Monique Show; also, worked with Monique's brother, producer, and manager. It was a pleasure working with them as they were both very intelligent, kind, loving and honest people to know and work with.

Mshiphopeffect

Candy Strother Devo

Candy with Stevie Wonder as Ms. Hip-hop Effect.

27

*Wayne Sheldon Perry an official photographer of
Face of Rap Mothers along with Eddie Bell Queen G's husband.*

Candy Strother DeVore Mitchell crew at an opener event.

Candy with friends from in the entertainment industry.

Lauren Graham of the Gilmore Girls on Warner Brothers
studio with Ricardo – image unpreserved.

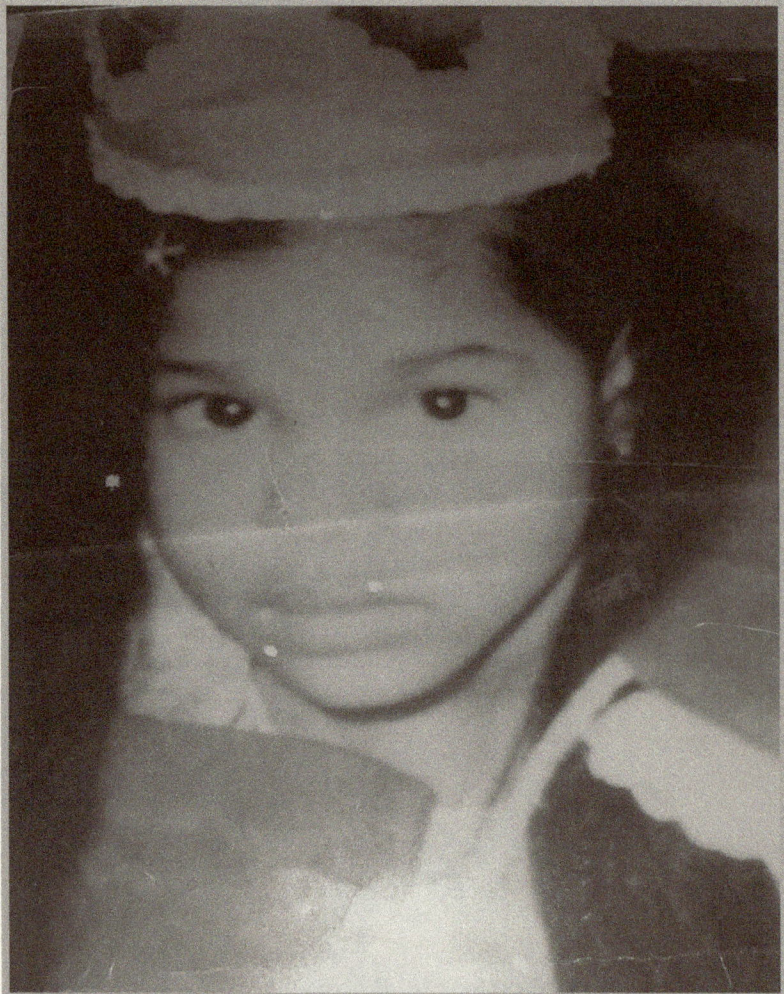

Candy's daughter Ricara Cheyenne Honey, now known as
West Coast Hip-hop Artist HONEY won the title of Lil Miss Los Angeles in 2002.

*Snoop Dogg's Uncle Don Juan with Freda on the
Bishop Don Juan Show, a long-time friend of Candy's.*

*Willie Lemon hip-hop star who performed, "Jailbait," is a long-time friend of
Candy's who used to open for Will Smith. New record is forthcoming.*

Candy's baby sister Ashley with her daughter Kyrah who is an actress, dancer, model, and vocalist who should air on the Faces of Rap Mothers Show!

Candy's and her sister Diana, raised with the same mother and Diana performed for a while with The Marvelettes.

Michael from Disney with Candy at event.

Candy and her father.

At Stevie Wonder's mother's pool during Stevie Wonders Birthday Bash.

KURUPT and Candy at an event.

*KING THA RAPPER & Superstar KURUPT of Tha Dogg Pound,
with his lil brother Roscoe of Tha Dogg Pound, Disney star and well-known
African American actor Darius Love and Stacy Kelly.*

*Mayor Rex Parris with Candy Strother DeVore Mitchell and her family, including
HONEY and KING THA RAPPER. Mayor Parris is a good friend of Candy's; and
this is taken right after her release from the hospital for cancer treatments.*

As a CEO running a record label for the largest distribution company worldwide you might just end up in court.

With Stevie Wonder.

Candy's son, Lawrence Lee, with Bobby Kristina.

KURUPT and KING THA RAPPER.

The beautiful Ricara Cheyenne aka HONEY.

35

KING THA RAPPER at Universal Studio recording hit song, Rollin with Roscoe of Tha Dogg Pound, S Kelly, Lil Mama & Candy Strother DeVore Mitchell too.

Tina Brown, Bobby Brown, and Candy Strother DeVore Mitchell.

KING THA RAPPER, Queen G, Candy & friend at event.

Roscoe and Candy.

Candy & friend.

Rap Artist HONEY.

Omar "Big O" Gooding with KING
THA RAPPER recording
his hit album, Ten Toes Down with
single No Sleep.

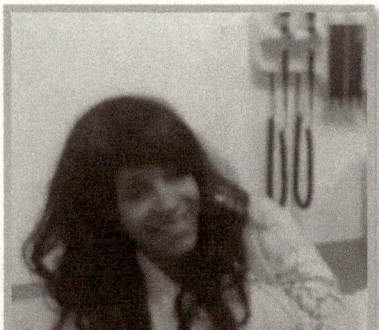

Candy getting cancer treatment at
Beverly Hills Hospital.
Take care of your health.

Candy with Carole Brown, Bobby Brown's sister. Bobby and Tommy, their
nephew Rapper T. Lahma were on the hit radio show, Shock Factor.

KING THA RAPPER at Universal Studios performing with
Omar Gooding, Roscoe, and McKinley, it was an awesome show.

Candy and KING live on the Queen G Live Experience Show in Las Vegas, Nevada.

KING, HONEY, Bobby Brown, Jr., Landon Brown, and Bobby Brown's 5-yr. old nephew Corey Brown

Candy Strother DeVore Mitchell on the news fighting for the best interest of children.

Ending human trafficking in-and-out of court, jurisprudence, and social platform systems where injustice prevails.

Candice in Atlanta, Georgia filming an episode of the Bobby Brown Family reality television show . . . stay tuned.

Candy and her children financed a Christmas toy & clothing giveaway for the less fortunate of Compton CA.
Featured here are some of the children receiving gifts with KING THA RAPPER and rap artist HONEY.

On break from filming the Bobby Brown Family Reality Show with Carole, Bobby's sister, and his niece.

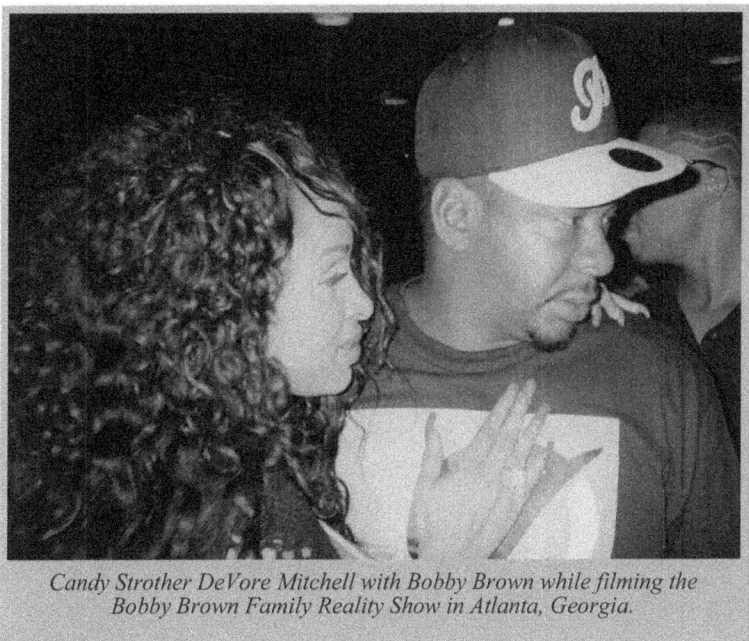

Candy Strother DeVore Mitchell with Bobby Brown while filming the Bobby Brown Family Reality Show in Atlanta, Georgia.

STARRING

LAST KINGS

KING THA RAPPER

BET★ Disney

FOR A FREE MP3 DOWNLOAD OF " POPULAR "
E-MAIL KINGTHARAPPERMUSIC@GMAIL.COM

Universal and Famous Records artist, KING THA RAPPER can be seen on Cartoon Network, Disney, MTV, and Nickelodeon.

CedAri Entertainment

PHARMACY

Universal and Famous Records artist, KING THA RAPPER can be seen on Cartoon Network, Disney, MTV, and Nickelodeon.

Roscoe and KING THA RAPPER of Tha Dogg Pound, filming the music video, Rollin. Models are Ricardo Cheyenne aka HONEY and her friend, hip-hop model Jeannie.

Shonta "Queen G" Gibson and Candy Strother DeVore Mitchell on the Queen G and Friends Radio Show.

Candy's daughter Ricardo Cheyenne aka Rapper HONEY on the music video set while filming.

Ricardo DeVore, Candy's son was the official clothing model for boxing legend Oscar Delahoya's clothing line; this image was taken working on the film set together.

KING THA RAPPER & KURUPT.

43

Jamie Paris, Candy Strother DeVore Mitchell, and
KING THA RAPPER at The Arsenio Hall Show.

Candy's mother Blanche Mitchell with Ricardo,
HONEY, Lawrence Lee, KING THA RAPPER, and
baby boy Hunter Jordan Lee.

KING THA RAPPER, Candy Strother DeVore Mitchell, with rap mother Berreta, her daughter Arelia, and Pam Bush with Craig Robinson who is a famous actor & comedian, backstage at Paramount Pictures.

*Taken on the film set of the Arsenio Hall Show. Rap Mothers Berreta and Candy were on the show with Berreta's daughter Arelia and Candy's son KING THA RAPPER at Universal Studios. They are featured with the mother of Superstar El Debarge - Gospel Great Etterlene Debarge.
The photo is taken on the stage set of the Arsenio Hall Show.
El Debarge had just given an amazing live performance.*

Will be available via Amazon

1ST BLACK FASHION MODEL IN THE U.S.A.

May 25

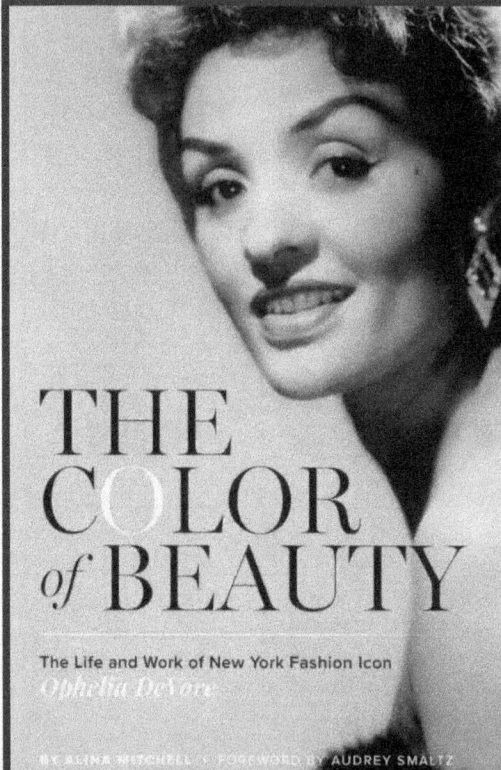

THE COLOR of BEAUTY

The Life and Work of New York Fashion Icon
Ophelia DeVore

BY ALINA MITCHELL | FOREWORD BY AUDREY SMALTZ

www.alinamakinimitchell.com
@alinamitchell writes

Dr. Ophelia DeVore-Mitchell, Candy's aunt has worked with four (4) of the United States Presidents, Bush, Carter, Ford, and Reagan. Candy's niece wrote this autobiography.

Superstar Bobby Brown's sister, famous award-winning author, and motivational speaker Leolah Brown Muhammad with Candy and close friends Iwana Cruz and her daughter Cocoa.

West Coast hip-hop artist HONEY is a Harvard University student and receives straight A's; she sets a good example for young adults.

West Coast female hip-hop Star Naturel Red and Superstar Bobby Brown's sister Carole Brown in the radio, at the radio station with Los Angeles famous DJ Crazy K.

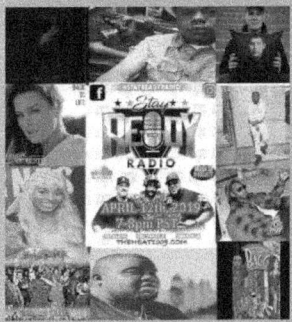

The Ready Radio.

Ophelia Devore marketed, managed, and promoted some of the biggest names in Hollywood. Auntie O represented Eartha Kitt and was very close friends with her. Diane Carol; Cecily Tyson and others visited Dr. DeVore as she built her start-up for charm, grace, image

47

334 Auburn Ave., N.E.

Southern Christian Leadership Conference

Martin Luther King Jr., *President*
Young, *Executive Director*

Ralph Abernathy, *Treasurer*

Andrew J.

July 17, 1967

Mrs Ophelia DeVore
Ophelia DeVore Associates, Inc
1697 Broadway
New York, New York

Dear Mrs DeVore:

I am writing you personally to express deep appreciation
for your generous contribution, but even more than that I
want to communicate thanks of the multitudes who benefit
from the work your support makes possible.

S C L C has continued adherence to Negro-white unity,
nonviolence and responsible militant action. We know these
principles have won landmark victories and will continue to
be effective tactics to realize justice and equality.

When our staff works in the rural South to register voters
or educate illiterates or when it organizes in the teeming
ghettos of the North, it is strengthened by the
undergirding of your support.

We are proud that you are one of us in this, the great
democratic crusade of our era. With warmest regards, I
am

Sincerely yours,

M King Jr.

Martin Luther King, Jr

MLK/o Enclosure: 1

A letter from Dr Martin Luther King, Jr. that she gave to me.
Dr. King gave my aunt deep appreciation for her work in civil rights.

KING THA
Rapper

1. Introduce yourself to the world?
My name is King Tha Rapper, I'm an 18 year old Rapper / Producer from Los Angeles, California who is currently signed to Capitol Music Group. You may know me from the work I did with Tha Dogg Pound, I am the youngest member of the D.P.G.

2. What inspired you to make music?
A lot of my family has been in the entertainment industry all my life. Growing up I was in studios, on film sets, shooting commercials, etc. etc. As I got older I just really took a passion to producing and I quickly realized I needed someone to make a song to my beats & that's when I decided to rap.

3. Tell everyone about your single with Kurupt?
In early 2015 I released a single entitled "I.M.O (In My Opinion)" featuring west coast rap legend and original member of "Tha Dogg Pound" Kurupt Young Gotti. The single received over 180k plays online & peaked #35 for five months straight on national airplay charts.

4. What do you want people to take home after experiencing a King The Rapper show?
When I perform I want people to take home a new favorite artist.

Issue 10 | 9

KING THA RAPPER and KURUPT of
Tha Dogg Pound featured in hip-hop magazines.

49

Candy Strother DeVore Mitchell's
Black Cash Universal Entertainment film and production company.

One of Candy's newest projects is Amerius Hudgins,
her nephew who is a New York rapper that is making
a lot of noise from New York to Miami.

Another of Candy's new projects
Dub Dub - TRS Team – promotions.

Another of Candy's newest
projects is her Latino nephew KP
who is a Puerto Rican and
Mexican rapper coming out of
Indiana. Look out for KPStyles
you will be hearing more of him.

KING THA RAPPER, KURUPT, Roscoe, and
Stacy Kelly – Tha Dogg Pound.

Set Shakur hugging her first cousin, Shantell.

Candy's Godmother, Tupac's brother & sister, Tyrone & Sekyiwa "Set" Shakur.

Candy, rapper, and hip-hop artist Havoc aka Mouthpiece of South-Central Cartel at the Poppas Kitchen with KING THA RAPPER filmed in the West Coast, starring Candy's children's Godfather TJ Pops Johnson.

West Coast Poppas Kitchen filming with KING THA RAPPER, Pops Johnson, Honey, Lawrence Lee, Timbo, Berreta, and Candy.

Meeting within the California Congress building to stop human trafficking of children in and out of foster care.

THE WHITE HOUSE
WASHINGTON

August 14, 2013

Ms. Ophelia DeVore
35 East 35th Street
New York, New York 10016

Dear Ophelia:

Happy 92nd birthday! We send our warmest wishes as you mark this special occasion.

Your extraordinary generation has steered America through trying times, shattered barriers, and helped lead our Nation into an era of progress and promise. As you celebrate this milestone, we hope you reflect with pride on your many contributions to the American story and on all you have accomplished over the course of your life.

We wish you all the best in the coming year.

Sincerely,

Michelle Obama

Dr Ophelia DeVore Mitchell was given this Birthday card from the White house President Barack Obama and his lovely wife Michelle.

Candy took this image of nephew Lashadion Anthony Shemwell her cousin, who was elected to office. Rolanda Greer proudly stands by her son as he makes history. Rolanda is an amazing singer who grew up living in the home with the Legendary superstar Marvin Gaye.

THE ORIGINAL MARVELETTES
(bottom Right) Lead Singer **Gladys Horton**
(Left) **Wanda Young** (Top) **Katherine Anderson**

The Original Marvelettes.

KING THA RAPPER - I.M.O. FT. KURUPT YOUNG GOTTI

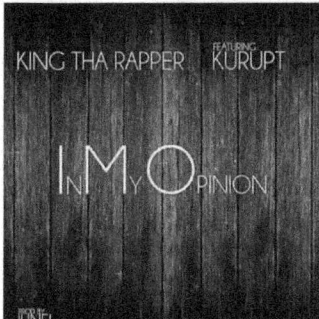

#	Artist	Title
55	KING THA RAPPER	I.M.O. IN MY OPINION FEAT KURUPT
56	LIFECHURCH	BEAUTIFUL HEART
57	U2	LOVE MY CHICK
58	AMIR	MAKE YOU PROUD
59	ACAPIXO	GO HEAD
60	MARCUS HUSTLE	MR. BRUNH
61	LUCKY HARMON	FAIRY OFF
62	MANI SORRI	LOST LOVE (DANCE REMIX)
63	J-CRAZY	THE LIFE
64	YOUNG JP	DIGITS
65	J-HEN	BYE CELEPSS
66	LAMAR JAY	LOVERBOY FT. SKEME
67	LEO WHITAKER	PLANTED BY THE WATER
68	GEO DAVIS	DAT CHECK
69	LUKE UNDERHILL	SOMETHING
70	FINDING LUCY	THIS TIME
71	ND	BALLING
72	KD ROSE	FALLING
73	TREL MAJOR	THE ROUTINE
74	P.J. PACIFICO	READY TO RUN
75	MARCUS RILEY	GIMMIE US
76	RODNEY MORSE	BORN IN AMERICA
77	LANKIN STYLE	RIGHT NOW
78	BIG T	AINT SHXT
79	DES M	O.D.P.E
80	LUKE UNDERHILL	STARS

In My Opinion – IMO – industry chart, etc.

55

Honey

2. What inspired you to start making music?
I was in a music group with my brothers when I was younger called "Devore Kids," but it wasn't really my focus. My brother, "King Tha Rapper" has always wanted to be a musician though, and in the spring of 2016 he was recording an EP and I was in the studio with him a lot. Witnessing the creative process with a close lens inspired me to give it a try.

3. How do you feel about today's hip-hop?
I feel like we are a funny generation. We're obviously inspired by the greats because of our parent's influence, but a lot of today's youth demean the old school because they don't realize the influences artist of the past have had on their favorite artist today. To keep it real, the OG's are the reason why we create art the way we do. I think there are a lot of talented musicians coming up now and we're witnessing history repeat the pattern of new legends emerging every generation.

4. What is next?
I'm working on an EP that will hopefully drop before the summer, as well as a longer mixtape by the end of the year. I'll be touring soon probably, and I'm also working on new music videos, getting back into acting, and am currently in the process of launching my fashion line. 2019 everything's taking off.

1. How did you get your name?
My name is Ricara Cheyenne Honee. So I've always been Honey. My grandmother called me that when I was little. I've also always been passionate about fashion, and a few years ago I told myself I would initially start my line. I asked my grandmother about name recommendations and she said "Honee," So after my grandma passed away and I started writing music, Honey just seemed natural. I changed the last "E" to a "Y" because I've always preferred that spelling.

@ricaracheyenne
ricaracheyenne
N/A
ricaracheyenne
Booking Email: officialhoneymusic@gmail.com

Hip-Hop and Rap Artist Honey magazine article.

Queen G Show advertisement.

HIPHOPMUZIKEFFECT-TV

HOLLYWOOD

HIP-HOP MUZIK EFFECT-TV w/Faces of Rap Mothers.

Dr. Ophelia Devore Mitchell with Past Presidents (Gerald Ford, Jimmy Carter, Ronald Reagan, George Bush)

Auntie O with President Gerald Ford, President Jimmy Carter, President Ronald Reagan and President Bush.

Strother

DeVore

Mitchell

Strother, DeVore and Mitchell Crests.

CHAPTER TWO
HONEY BLUNT

Honey Blunt - six-time award-winning rap and hip-hop artist. When Honey Blunt left Arkansas, she headed to California, pursuing a career in rap and Hip-hop. She met, worked with, and befriended Jayceon Terrell Taylor better known as "The Game," which was a great decision because Jayceon treated Honey like family, encouraging her startup . . . resulting in meeting and marrying Blunt West Entertainment CEO, John L. Blunt.

THIS TALENTED LADY IS A SUCCESSFUL MODEL who has filmed several hip-hop movies and performed nationally and within, Los Angeles as a rapper. Honey, an active commentator on *Face of Rap Mothers Show*, hails from Arkansas and is a "now" six (6) time award-winning *West Coast* recording artist. As an actress, businesswoman, and model; *Honey* is also "*a mom.*" Understandably, with three (3) lovely children, and a decent performance calendar . . . this rap and hip-hop star shares solid strength of character alongside her husband . . . Mr. John L. Blunt, Chief Executive Officer (CEO) of *Blunt West Entertainment*. As *Honey's* production manager, John pitch-hits as a co-equal and these two parents hold it down with qualitative success. Further, Honey assists John, with the entertainment organization and this combination of talent promotes the Blunt family's successes. Having recorded, and performed, with *Keenon Daequan Ray Jackson* better known as *Superstar Rapper "YG"*, Honey *also has* performed with an abundance of extremely well-recognized and applauded rap and hip-hop artists, which demonstrates her level of success.

Recently, awarded titles at *Best West Coast Female Rapper* event – Honey holds the title of *#1 of Queens of West Coast Rap*; she was also awarded at *Soul Central Awards* and has been featured in numerous rap and hip-hop magazines and cast in motion picture roles as well.

Soul Central Awards 2019/20 – Honey Blunt Awarded

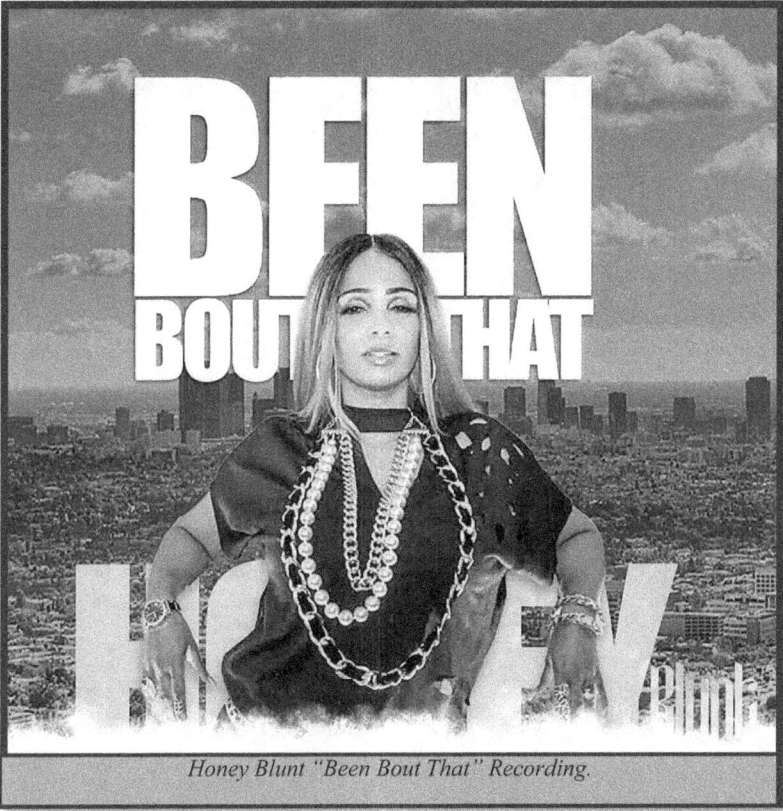

Honey Blunt "Been Bout That" Recording.

Honey Blunt Rockin' Shades.

Honey Blunt on stage.

Honey Blunt and Family.

John Blunt and Children.

Honey, John & Son.

Honey & John's Son.

Honey Blunt & Son.

Blunt Family.

Honey Blunt.

Honey Blunt Soul Central Story.

Honey Blunt & Queen G - Vegas.

Honey Performance Live Performance Poster.

Honey Blunt.

Honey Blunt Untouchable Magazine.

Honey showing some love.

John Blunt holding awards.

Honey Blunt Modeling.

Honey Blunt Performers.

Honey on stage.

Honey & Performers.

Honey Blunt & Celebrities.

Honey &Theater Troupe.

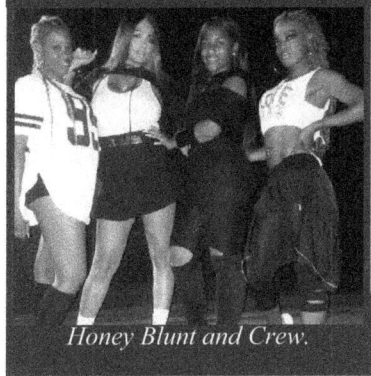

Honey Blunt and Crew.

65

Honey Blunt.

Honey Blunt & Crew.

Diva Honey with husband John.

Honey Blunt with family.

CHAPTER THREE
MONICA DAVIS

Monica Davis (Monica Monae) – 26 May 1967.

MY NAME IS MONICA DAVIS aka Monica Monae. I was born in Los Angeles (LA), 26 May 1967. My parents, Barry, and Freda Davis, whom I love, raised me in Baldwin Hills where I graduated from *Baldwin Hills Elementary*. We moved from there to Inglewood. I attended *Crozer Junior High* in Inglewood. Shortly thereafter, we moved to San Diego, where I attended *Mira Mesa High School*. Upon graduation,

67

I took a detour back to LA and met my BFF, *Candy Strother DeVore-Mitchell* while there.

Candy and I were inseparable. Every concert in LA we attended and were invited backstage. We were blessed to have the opportunity to attend celebrity parties and events. Eventually, after I moved back to San Diego, Candy visited with *Eazy-E* and *Chico DeBarge*. Candy made certain I knew San Diego, at only two and a half hours away, was just around the corner. We had a blast together, and she remains my BFF!

After some time passed, I once again returned to LA to live. Candy had a bunch of fun things lined up for us to do. We went to Stevie Wonder's birthday party and hung out with *Bobby Brown, El DeBarge, Fat Boys, Johnny Gill, LL Cool J, Maserati, New Edition,* and *Run DMC* to name just a few. We also hung out at *Ralph Tresvant's* home almost daily, and chilled with his Uncle Derick, and his mother Trish. We practically lived at Franklin Plaza – our old stomping grounds. Franklin Plaza was a hotel that resembled an apartment complex, and celebrities stayed at Franklin when they held events in LA.

After a while, I met and dated *Jesse D* from the R&B group *Force MD* and started a group, *LACE*, which consisted of Candy, Sheryl, and I. Joe Jackson, and his assistant, John Wilson collaborated with us and set us up with writers and producers. I recollect one occasion where Candy, Sheryl, and I were sitting in the hotel room with *Toni Toni Toni* who were giving us the lowdown regarding the music business. They told us to stay focused and keep a tough skin. Unfortunately, at the time, we could not keep our group going. We were being pulled in different directions as artists, and as individuals. One of us wanted to sing lead on everything. One of us wanted to do most of the writing and another of us wanted to be a choreographer. We were doomed from the Gitty-Up . . . LMBO. Like many young adults . . . we did not have the brains . . . but we did have the beauty!

As that chapter of my life closed, I married and soon had a baby boy who is all grown up and living in Belize at this time. I divorced, and then remarried to R&B musician *Dwayne Jones* from the group, *Single*. At the time, they were touring with *Destiny's Child* and maintaining our marriage was not easy. I was not strong enough to hold onto what became a toxic relationship. I soon restructured my life and relocated to Houston Texas. I am now employed in the nursing industry in Houston and work with adolescents in psyche settings. I have the capability to share love and caring with youth who experience mental disability, and I enjoy what I do. While my own son is not a rapper, I embrace the rap and hip-hop industry and Candy was kind to include me as a contributor in her book. Today, I remain a nurturer caring for humanity. Growing up with *Candy Strother DeVore-Mitchell* as my best friend - more of a sister – remains a blessing in my life. I am her son *KING THA RAPPER's* Godmother and could not ask for anything more from a good friend. She introduced me to entertainers and a world of fun. We have had opportunities to travel everywhere together and enjoy our lives. I thank GOD for that.

Even if I do not go anywhere new or unusual again in my lifetime – I have had fun in the sun with my best friend, *Candy Strother DeVore-Mitchell* - I am happy to share my story in the *Faces of Rap Mothers*.

Monica Davis.

Monica Davis.

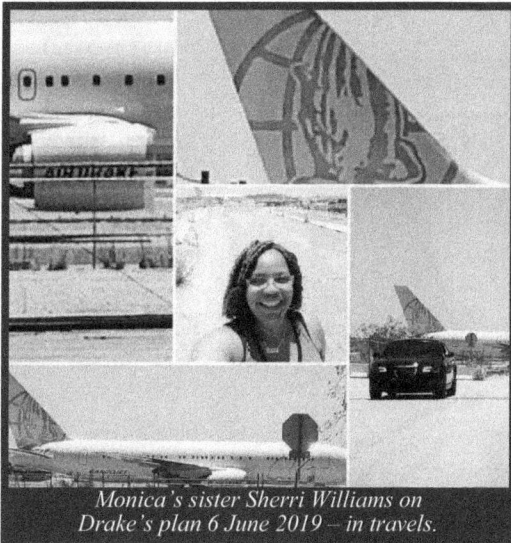

Monica's sister Sherri Williams on Drake's plan 6 June 2019 – in travels.

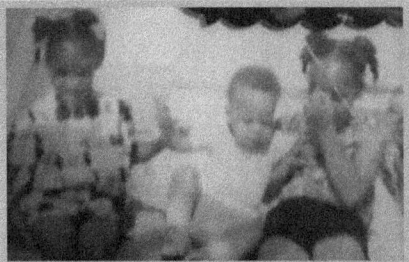

Monica, her sister Sherri and baby brother Barry Davis, Jr. Sister.

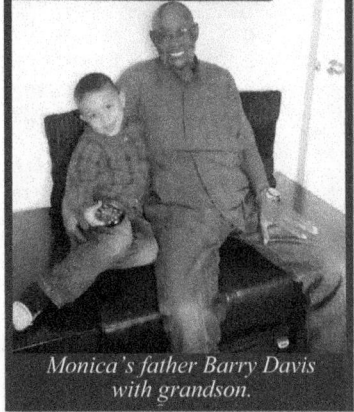

Monica's father Barry Davis with grandson.

Monica with her mother and sister.

Monica with her sister.

Monica Davis.

CHAPTER FOUR
SHONTA GIBSON (QUEEN "G")

Shonta Gibson is an award-winning media Queen referred to as Queen G. She grew up in Watts, California with hip-hop brother, Superstar Tyrese Gibson, who also has many movie credits including The Fast & The Furious. Queen G runs her own company, "Let's Go to Work Entertainment."

MY NAME IS SHONTA RENEE GIBSON, aka Queen G. I fell love with media early in my life, in my twenties. At that time, I owned a magazine titled, *77 Magazine*, which was an entrepreneurial entertainment magazine featuring up-and-coming talent within Los Angeles. As Editor-in-Chief, I conducted interviews, and was blessed to interview stellar talents, such as *Affion Crockett, Tarajii Henson and Katt Williams* to name just a few.

In addition to folks like these, I was able to interview my brother, Tyrese Gibson who landed a cover. Of course, as a musician, and actor, my brother is well-recognized within the entertainment industry and that boosted *77 Magazine* tremendously. Thus, began a career for me that has spanned the many years of my life.

Some challenges, everyone has them, resulted in my taking a two-year sabbatical where I reinvigorated myself before returning even stronger. When readied, I began a new business, *Edgelight Entertainment* in Westchester California in a small office on the building's top floor.

When I was handed the keys to my new office – the realization I was starting a new business struck me - I did not know what I was going to do in that office, but it resulted in history being made in a short amount of time. It started with promotions for local Los Angeles clubs – where I was paid to invite clients to events and that really paid off. I loved entertaining guests and being paid to pack clubs with customers. It was not work as much as it was fun. Networking was natural to me. I was blessed to have opportunity to gain experience about many diverse types of people while conducting business. And, knowing a wide expanse of people without judgment, with a lens toward the future, is as essential as it is fun, at least, it was for me.

Once *Edgelight* was off the ground – I began project casting through my office. A friend, Keith Adams requested I cast his sitcoms. I agreed and successfully cast, *Me and My Old Man* where I was debuted as an actress in the show. When *Me and My Old Man* wrapped, I aspired to my next project, which was a movie titled, *Death by Association* written by *Jaytee Thompson* and directed by *Reuben Johnson*.

Casting this movie was a little more difficult because forty (40) actors were required, and filming was in separate locations; I managed to lockin the entire cast, which included *Tyrone Burton, Holmes Lindsey* and *Kisha Simone* among many other talented actors. By the grace of God, the movie was a success.

Afterward, I was provided an additional opportunity to act in *The Rap Game*, which resulted in celebrity interests. Actors such as, *Kiki Haynes Bell, Dubb C., Ken Lawson, and Vincent M Ward* were signed. It was a fun time in my life. I knew my career choices were solid. *The Rap Game*, as a production was never completed, but it prompted my initial recognition and paycheck. I must admit that felt powerful.

Projects continued to present themselves, including a patriotic music video titled, *America Standing Proud*. The children of veterans were required along with adults for the music video. It was a genuine production that paid well and offered me another small acting role. Written and directed by *Matt and Denise Demars*, the video was a success.

Shortly after this time, my life took another turn when I met a beautiful woman named *Carla Simpson*. She was the owner of *Entrepreneurs on The Move (EOTM)*, a multimillion-dollar company. When she inquired if I would agree to be a special guest on her radio program, I accepted. It was extremely exciting to be on her radio show and know that she thought enough of me to highlight me and my company. Amazing things were happening. Our interview went well. I was quite happy about the responses to her questions – you never really know how well an interview will be until it occurs. I knew we exchanged some synergy, but I did not know it was the beginning of my media mogul history. Shortly after the interview, Carla and I became close friends, I began referring celebrity friends to be interviewed by radio personalities she featured on her program. This created an entire new swim lane of business for me and resulted in another media outlet that expanded business reach.

Each interview request I presented to Carla resulted in interviews. She never turned down one of my referrals. She always made space for my clients. Eventually, she offered me my own show and while a humbling experience due to the fact she thought enough of me to make the offer, I was ecstatic. Immediately, I began the creation process for a program name, as all the hosts on *EOTM* had great program names, which flowed with their personalities.

Carla shared with me, "You seem like Queen G to me."

I responded, "There it is."

I have been called Queen G ever since that time.

So, my radio program became the "Queen G Show." I could not believe I had my own radio program. Right away, I was introduced to carpet-hosting and was out there getting interviews. I must admit the experience was frightening, and exciting, simultaneously. Since my first radio platform with *EOTM*, I have co-hosted, and hosted, many radio shows. Eventually, I became a media teacher and developed "The Queen G Media Course."

Some of the entertainers I have interviewed include *Rob Base, Buschwhick Bill* (God rest his soul), *Dana Dana, Flava Flav, Salt N Pepa, Teddy Riley, Too Short, SMV, Paul Wall, Keith Washington, Az Yet,* and others.

In closing, I want to thank you for taking time out of your busy life to share a brief snapshot into my history that I am going to expand on in a future book release. Currently, my work is available on all platforms under *Queen G's Live Experience.*

Additionally, I want to give a big shout out and thank you to my husband Eddie Bell. He holds me down with the camera daily. Also, I want to share the love I carry for my eight (8) children Tanisha, Star, Savon, Madison, Eric, Heaven, Divinity and Serenity and my three grandchildren Allayah, Isaiah and September.

And, of course, I cannot forget to mention my dear parents – Tyrone and Priscilla and my siblings Salendra, Tyrone, Tyrese, and Nyesha. I love my entire family with my every breath.

Lastly, most important to me is the thanks I give to God for keeping me and providing a life path within the media industry for me and my family. Thank you, God, for ordering my steps daily.

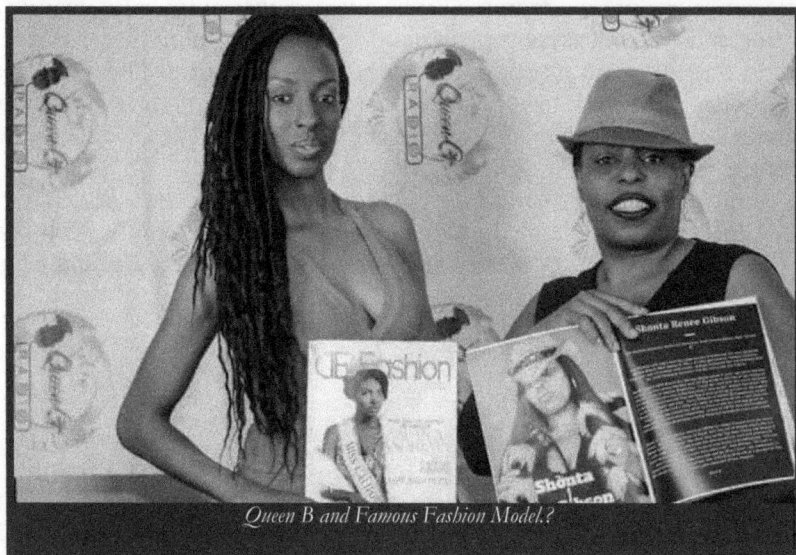

Queen B and Famous Fashion Model.?

Shonta "Queen G" Gibson.

Las Vegas Power Couple
Eddie Bell & Shonta Gibson

Letsgotowork Entertainment is a new age innovative branding and marketing company that gets behind the brand of those that they touch. Their edgy style of PR, Promo Videos, Marketing, and branding boosts the sales, traffic, and visibility of every brand that they touch. Letsgotowork was created by Shonta Gibson and Eddie Bell a hus-

band and wife duo that has history in the entertainment industry that spans over 20 years.

They are a powerhouse force in the industry that turns everything that they touch into gold.

Letsgotowork Entertainment Provides media Marketing, photography, videography, and branding. They also do exclusive interviews, red carpet hosting and events Be on the lookout for them, they are a force to be reckoned with.

Social Media Links
Facebook: Let's Gotswork Entertainment Network
website: Lgonlive.com

Shonta Gibson & Flavor Flav

Eddie Bell with T.I.

Nubian Empire Magazine

Las Vegas Power Couple Story featuring Eddie Bell and Shonta Gibson (Queen G).

Shonta Gibson, SMW and Salt-N-Pepa.

Queen G and Salt-N-Pepa.

Queen G and All 4 1.

Queen G.

Soul Central Magazine.

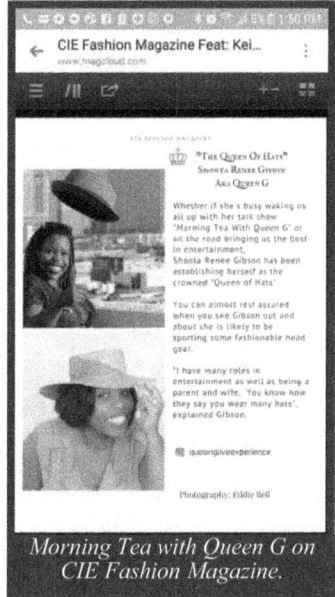

Morning Tea with Queen G on
CIE Fashion Magazine.

Queen G - On The Rise.

Shonta Gibson &
her brother
Superstar Tyrese Gibson.

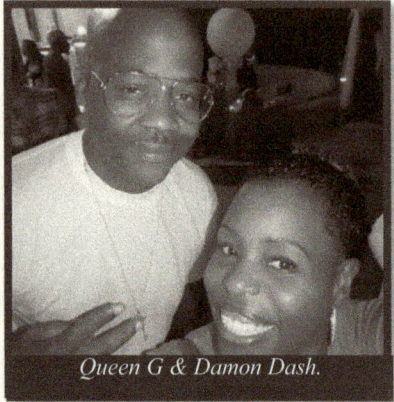

Queen G & Damon Dash.

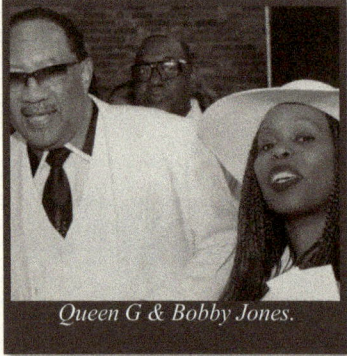

Queen G & Bobby Jones.

Queen G & Raz B.

Queen G & Damien Hall.

Queen G & Keith Washington.

Queen G & Spice 1.

Queen G & After 7.

Queen G & Spice 1 and Buschwhick Bill.

*Queen G &
Superstar Rapper T.I.*

Actor Tyrese Gibson's Sister Queen G.

Queen G & Teddy Riley.

Queen G & Flava Flav.

SERRA MANUFACTURING CORP.
Vincent M. Ward.

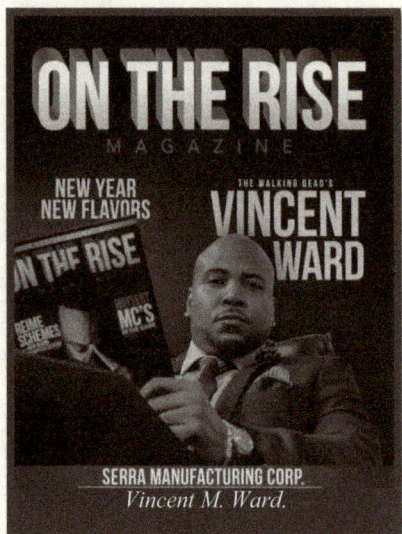
Queen G & Heavy D.

Queen G – Shonta Gibson.

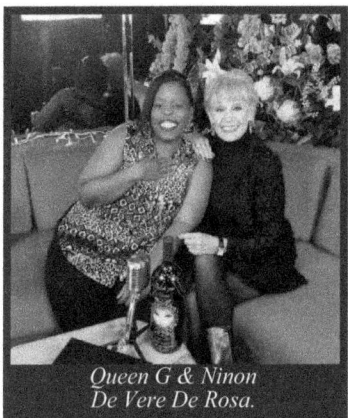

Queen G & Ninon De Vere De Rosa.

Eddie Bell and Paul Wallwith.

Queen G & Dizzy Wright.

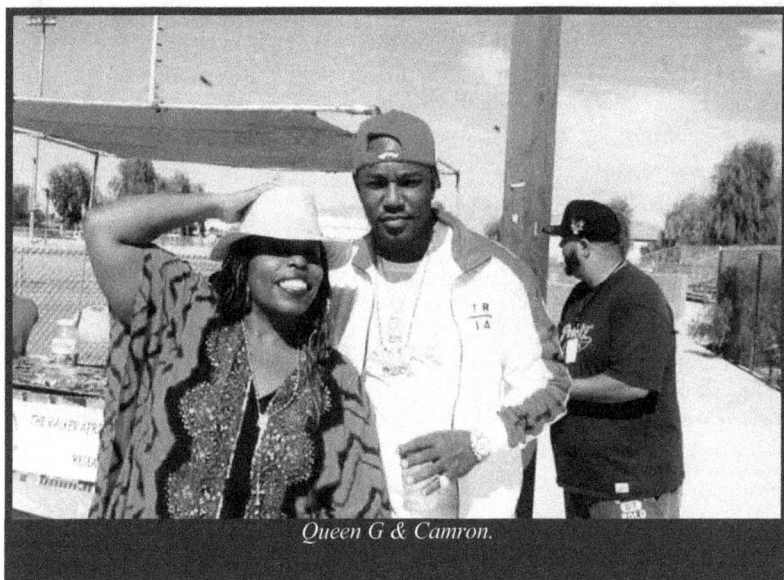

Queen G & Camron.

ACTRESS

2018 Addict 2018
2018 Is That Man Your Husband?
2008 Me and My Old Man (Short)

CASTING

2008 Common Bond (Short) (casting associate)

PRODUCER

2008 Me and My Old Man (Short) (associate producer)

THANKS

2008 Common Bond (Short) (thank you)

SELF

2011 E! Buzz with Carla B (Short)

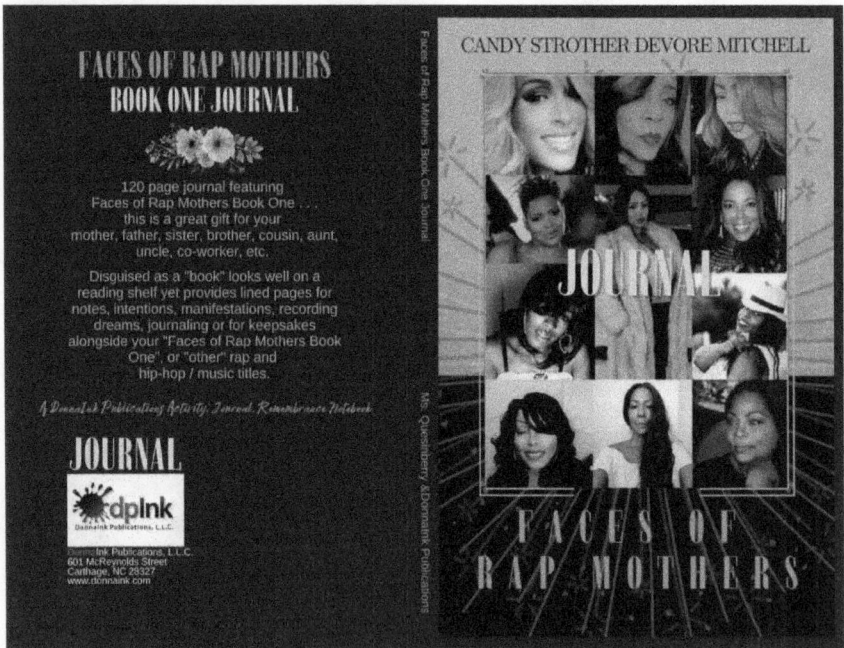

CHAPTER FIVE
ANGELA GILCHRIST-GUYTON

Angela Gilchrist Guyton

WHERE DO I BEGIN? I THINK IT'S SAFE to begin when I first met Guy Mitchell, who I married, and who became the father of our son Guy Mitchell Jr., III. Introduced through a close acquaintance in the late 80's for the purpose of music, I was flattered Guy took an interest in me, and the manner he went about pursuing me. He brought flowers to me every day from the day we met, until the day he asked me to be his wife. *Can you imagine?* I had never experienced anyone so serious in making an honest woman out of me, like *Guy*. We fell in love instantly. The moment he asked me to consider what it sounded like to be called, Mrs. Angela Mitchell stuck to my heart like glue. Three months after we met, we ran off quietly to get married. We honeymooned, and traveled to, the Bahamas, on a routine basis, as if it were a second home away from home. Atlanta, GA is where we resided while married for the eleven (11) years we were.

Our son Guy Mitchell Jr., III was born not long after we were married, Guy Sr. was an impressive provider, and an excellent father to our son. He worked his professional office job, and ran our detail cleaning service, and the music studio. I called him "workaholic." He worked so hard, I almost lost him to a heart attack, twice. That really shook me, and the family, up terribly. We worked closely together in the studio, and collaborated on songs together, like *Ashford and Simpson.* I was his personal singer and songwriter – we were *Solid As A Rock.*

To this day, *Guy* is one of the *best of the best* when it comes to producing. He's worked with the famously known *Bobby Brown, Peabo Bryson* (where I personally watched him sing live in his recording sessions of the hit song *Can You Stop The Rain*), *Mariah Carey, The Deuce* (whom I've personally sang backup and did a *Mothers Against Drunk Driving* commercial with as an extra), *TLC*, and *Usher.*

I grew extremely attached to *Peabo* while collaborating with him in his sessions. He nicknamed me *Baby Girl* and spoiled me like a daughter whenever I had come with *Guy* to his sessions. He said, "You remind me of my daughter, you are the "only" other person that will boldly tell me about my bad cigarette habit." Can you believe it? With a voice like his? It bothered me, because my husband had to work in that environment, and somebody had to stand up and say something. And I couldn't breathe either, LOL! Granted it was *Peabo's* paid for session, but you know how us women can be overly protective of our husbands.

Somewhere down the line, *Guy* and I grew apart and moved in separate directions, we went our separate ways, but we remained good friends . . . feeling it best for our son to remain cordial and be friends.

A little about me, first - I am a mixed breed – my mother Ellenore Gilchrist who is no longer with me in this world, was born in Germany and raised there until about ten (10) years of age until she came to America. She was my biggest fan. Everything in my music career was for her. On her side, we are German, Irish, and Japanese. My daddy, Willie Guyton was Black. Our folks from his line, come from Mississippi and New Orleans. My youngest daughter Nya calls us *GERBLASIANS* = German, Black and Asian.

Currently, I have four (4) grown children who live independently, with exception of my youngest daughter, Nya. My children's names are De'Juan, Guy Jr, Marissa and Nya and they are all exceptionally talented. De'Juan is a formidable artist, my son Guy is also an impressive artist and rapper, my eldest daughter Marissa is a model and artist as well as my youngest, Nya who is an up-and-coming singer. She is looking forward to collaborating with my sister-in-law, Candice's daughter HONEY as she begins working on her new album soon. I have three (3) grandchildren Devyn, Jaylen, and Leighani. They are my joy and my world. It melts my heart to hear them call me *Oma* (German for grandmother). There are no words to describe the love for your grandchildren. It is truly humbling, and a blessing!

I realized I had talent around the fourth grade. I entered talent shows and could not get enough of them. I began dancing in talent shows before I realized I could sing, which came to me at about the sixth grade. My sisters, Kris, and Lisa, and I performed in my parents living room while they were away for work. We pretended we were the group *Sister Sledge*, Lol! My sisters did not continue with singing, but I had a bug for it. I have sung ever since. I started rehearsing with my Aunt *Shirley Cartman* who started a group called *The New Generation Band* in the late 80's.

My Aunt Shirley was also the author of a book titled, *A Teacher Remembers the Jackson's*. In the book, she talks about when she was a music teacher at Roosevelt High School in Gary Indiana where the *Jackson's* attended. Aunt Shirley could play about any instrument and was a fine teacher. *Joe Jackson* got in touch with her to teach the Jackson boys how to play guitar and they came over to rehearse every Saturday before they became famous. At that time, my mother and I lived in the basement apartment. I was just a toddler still.

My mother told me many stories of the Jackson boys and how they used to come over for rehearsals. She said she and her cousin Joy Riley-Cartman were the cookie and Kool aid makers for the Jacksons. She shared how Michael would come to my playpen to play with me as a young boy. Michael would say, "I have a baby sister at home the same age as she is." He was referring to Janet at the time; she said they were very humble children, and fun to be around.

Growing up, I had the pleasure of listening to their rehearsals when I got involved with my aunt's group, *The New Generation Band*. She invited us over for family gatherings and showed us pictures while allowing us to hear audios she had of the Jackson boys' rehearsals. After the Jackson's became big and famous, she was reunited with them on the news in Atlanta on their *Victory Tour*. She was invited backstage and had the chance to see them perform. She said she could not describe what she felt seeing them perform from when they rehearsed in her basement. She felt happy and sad because she thought they were like prisoners in public life. She knew they could not go anywhere without bodyguards.

A couple of years later, I ran into a group called, *The Mystic Allstar Steel Band* by accident at a Jamaican food store. I heard the most beautiful sounds coming from the back of the warehouse of the store – the steel drums – I asked at the front who, what, and where the music was coming from? She invited me to sit and watch the group rehearse. I was HOOK-ED! I could not help myself. When I walked over to the drummer, due to his style and technique and how he played Calypso, I was doubly hooked. He was BAD! I was so into his style of playing. After the song was over, the drummer known as Francis said to me in a Trinidad voice, "Come darling, you can do this too." I was shy about playing drums, so I resisted, but he insisted.

He showed me a few techniques I caught onto very quickly. Before I knew it, I was in every rehearsal from there on. I became so good they made me a part of the band. I substituted for Francis when he needed to take breaks. People do not realize how much of a physical demand it is for a drummer to play an hour or two. Whooh, it can take a lot out of you. I traveled to many states in the south and played on many military bases and beach functions with *The Mystic Allstar Steel Band*. I had the time of my life and was only sixteen (16) and seventeen (17) working with the group before they moved on to other things. It was heartbreaking for me that they separated.

After I met my husband Guy Mitchell, I began recording profess-sionally in the studio as a solo artist with him. We had many songs that should have been released but if just did not happen. It was not the time. One song he and I wrote, gained radio airtime in five (5) different states across the United States was titled, *Never Give Up*. We received a lot of feedback on the song asking what inspired us. It was an inspirational song that *Peabo Bryson* asked me to write with *Martin Luther King* loops in the song from his *I Have A Dream* speech and Martin's son even suggested using it as a theme song for Martin Luther's birthday. Later, after Guy and I went our separate ways, I went to a club in Lawrenceville GA, where I met Tom from the 90's hip-hop group called, *Level III*.

At the time, my sister Lisa and I stepped into the club, it was like a music video. I was grabbed by the arm and asked by Tom if he could talk to me for a few minutes. I was captivated by his charm from that very minute. He was a perfect gentleman and properly introduced himself. I fell for him instantly; he looked familiar to me, but I did not recognize with whom I was talking. I remember seeing the video, which can be seen on YouTube now, but it did not connect in my brain. He remained in silence concerning his fame until the next day he invited me to a function he was having at his family's apartment. It was then, when I saw the poster and pictures framed on the wall on their hit song, *Groove Ya*, that I was both shocked, and embarrassed, for not knowing who they were, LOL!

You see *Level III* consisted of twins and their brother. Tom and his brother Marvin were the twins along with their brother. At the time, we were at the club, Tom mentioned to me he had a twin brother. I pardoned myself for a moment to get my sister Lisa to introduce to Tom. When they were introduced, Tom contacted his brother Marvin and invited us to his family function the next day to meet Marvin. After that, my sister Lisa and Marvin fell hard for each other and Tom and I as well - we were all inseparable. We had the time of our lives before they moved further down south. Lisa remained in Atlanta, and I moved to the East Coast.

Lisa took my old job as a supervisor at the Atlanta Hartsfield Airport in one of their gift shops. While working there she was approached by *Tupac* and they exchanged numbers. Before I left for the East Coast, Lisa and I would be home, the phone would ring, and it was always *Tupac* calling to speak with Lisa. He was famous for eating and chewing on something when he called. They were always on the phone and talked for hours. At first, I tried convincing her not to get too hooked on him because I always feared something bad would happen. Call me clairvoyant, but I just felt it in my gut.

Do not get me wrong, I love and miss *Tupac* as a person, a rapper, and entertainer. He was one of the best rappers I have ever heard, with some deep lyrics educating folks. But something about him expressing he knew he was gonna die young concerned me. I always felt he was a great contribution to the rap industry. He is deeply missed!

After I left Atlanta, Lisa called me in tears asking if I was watching the news and had heard what had just taken place. I could hear the devastation in her voice. I almost knew before she could tell me, it had something to do with *Tupac*. I turned on my television and could not believe my eyes and ears - the worst of which she was calling me about. She cried so hard while saying they killed her baby *Tupac*. My heart dropped, and all I could do was be there for her through the agony she was enduring.

Since I have been on the East Coast, I continue to pursue my music career. I have sung hooks, and backup, with many local rappers and artists. One of which I am in a music video on Youtube with, is the up and rising group, *G.M.B (Get Money Brother's)*. The name of the song on Youtube is, *G.M.B's We On Top*. I have done a few other songs with them that are on their CD titled, *Murking Season*.

I always wanted to get into film, and was approached by independent film producer, *Daniel Primo Live Glen* who asked me to play a role in, *Mad City*, which can be found on YouTube. I agreed and played a victim to the lead. Currently, I am again working with Daniel on another lead in the movie, *Mambo Sauce*.

Daniel is incredibly talented and creative. I am looking forward to collaborating with him more in the future as he continues to develop and grow his name. I am sure you will all get to know more about his work very soon.

I have had a very fulfilling, fun, and interesting life up to now and my life is just beginning!

Angela Gilchrist-Guyton

Angela's first husband, Candy Strother DeVore Mitchell's brother Edward Guy Mitchell, an entertainment producer of the stars, known for platinum & gold recordings where he worked with artists such as Marah Carey, Alesha Keys, Usher, TLC, SOS Band, The Commodores, etc. Guy has produced alongside some of the greatest music producers such as Jermaine Dupree.

De'Juan Mitchell – Angela Gilchrist Guyton, and Guy Mitchell Sr.'s, son with his lovely wife.

Guy Mitchell, Jr. III – son of Guy Mitchell, Jr. II and Angela Gilchrist-Guyton; also, Candy Strother DeVore Mitchell's nephew.

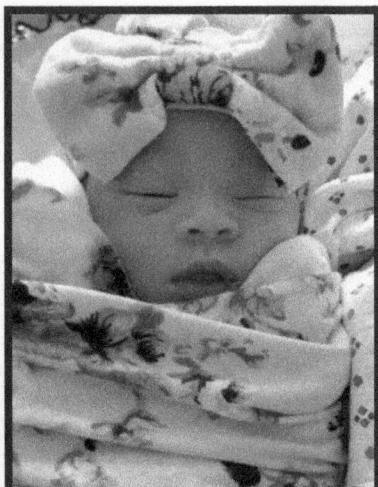

Angela Gilchrist-Guyton's grandchildren courtesy of eldest son De'Juan, and eldest daughter Marissa. Angela is referred to as "Oma" referencing her Germanic roots from her mother.

Angela recording.

Angela modeling Team Fault Line for OG DUV MAC Dogg's clothing line.

Guy Mitchell, Jr. III modeling.

Guy Mitchell Sr. and Jr. on Father's Day.

Angela's youngest daughter Nya.

Model and beauty pageant winner.
Photo Credit: Zeamera.

Angela's sister Lisa
who fell in love with Tupac.

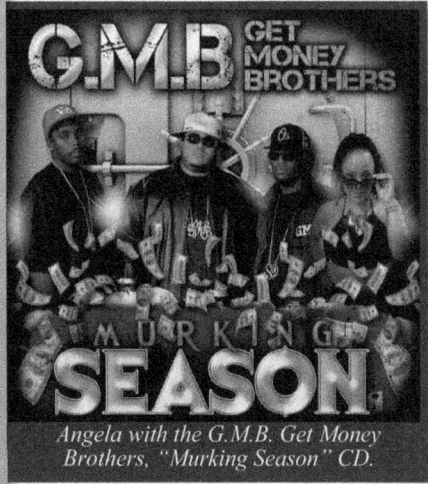

Angela with the G.M.B. Get Money
Brothers, "Murking Season" CD.

Angela's striking beauty.

Guy Mitchell Jr., III.

From left to right and top to bottom,
Angela's daughters Nya and Marissa.

A picture from a scene from the movie Mad City.

Angela's baby daughter, Nya a lovely singer like her mother

Daniel Primo Live Glenn

Another scene from the movie Mad City.

CHAPTER SIX
TYAUNNA HARRIS

*Tyaunna Harris
hip-hop Model & Video Queen.*

TYAUNNA HARRIS IS A WELL-KNOWN hip-hop model and reality TV actress. Her mother, the wonderful Carla Ann Flowers, supported her beautiful daughter's modeling and acting career choices. Tyaunna also has performed in several rap and hip-hop videos.

Tyaunna Harris and her children.

Tyaunna Harris – hip-hop Video Actress.

Tyaunna Harris – hip-hop Model.

Tyaunna Harris Family.

Tyaunna Harris Model.

Tyaunna Harris and her mother.

Tyaunna Harris, Candy and son Lawrence.

CHAPTER SEVEN
ANGELA HICKS

Angela Hicks – O.G. Lil Mama

ANGELA HICKS, KNOWN AS O.G. LIL MAMA in the hip-hop world, is a true entrepreneur. She loves God, music, and her craft. She creates her own jewelry, crochets (skull caps, beanies, and floppy hats), she dances, is a licensed hair stylist, she raps, sings, writes music, and is in the process of creating her own clothing line.

Known for being the one to go to when you need to reach someone else in the rap and/or hip-hop industry; Angela is the go-between who has been responsible for many connections between artists in the rap and hip-hop arena. If you cannot reach someone, they tell you, "Go call Lil Mama. She knows everyone."

Angela believes in helping anyone and everyone. She never hesitates to be the first in line to help you. In times of need, she is there for you. If you need advice, a couch to crash on, a home cooked meal, homie hook-up, a motivator or inspirator, a prayer warrior, a shoulder to cry on - she is the one to go to.

Angela does all these things without hesitation or reservation. She does all the things a mother would do for her children – for her friends. Angela is, and has been, a "mother figure" to many rap and hip-hop artists. She enjoys the role and is grateful to have been a blessing for so many. She loves her title of "Lil Mama" or "Auntie" as she is sometimes called. Angela is respected, looked up to, appreciated and admired by all whose lives she has touched.

O.G. Lil Mama and
Godbrother Snoop Dogg.

O.G. Lil Mama and
Sean Corey Carter aka Jay-Z.

O.G. Lil Mama and Superstar Rapper Ice Cube.

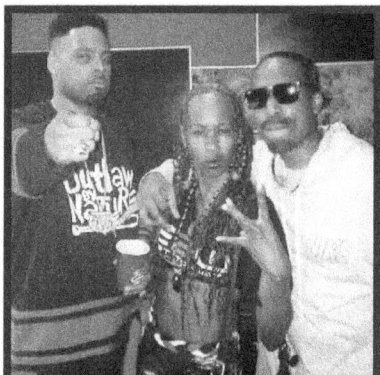

O.G. Lil Mama and KURUPT of the Dogg Pound.

O.G. Lil Mama and Superstar Producer/Rapper Dr. Dre.

O.G. Lil Mama and Superstar Tyrese Gibson's sister Shonta Renee.

O.G. Lil Mama and Superstar Rapper Nipsey Hussle.

O.G. Lil Mama, KURUPT & his younger brother Roscoe. All are members of Snoop Dogg's Tha Dogg Pound.

103

O.G. Lil Mama and Superstar Rapper DJ Quick.

O.G. Lil Mama and Superstar Friends.

O.G. Lil Mama and Superstar Red Man.

Angela Hicks – O.G. Lil Mama and her mother.

O.G. Lil Mama and Superstar Will Smith.

At Off The Planet Studio with KURUPT, KING THA RAPPER, Candy, and Lawrence Lee.

O.G. Lil Mama and Superstar Nate Dogg.

O.G. Lil Mama and Superstar Rapper DAZ.

O.G. Lil Mama and Superstar Nipsey Hussle.

O.G. Lil Mama and E40 of Tha Dogg Pound.

O.G. Lil Mama and Superstar Snoop Dogg.

105

O.G. Lil Mama and
Famous comedian / actress Kim Whitley.

O.G. Lil Mama and
Superstar Rapper Busta Rhymes.

O.G. Lil Mama
and LL Cool J.

O.G. Lil Mama
and KING THA RAPPER.

O.G. Lil Mama & Tina Brown, Candy,
Towanda Warren Close & her pops.

O.G. Lil Mama and
Superstar Bone Thugs N Harmony.

Either Your With Me Our Against ME

Angela Hicks
O.G. Lil Mama.

O.G. Lil Mama and
Tha Dogg Pound.

O.G. Lil Mama and
Superstar Rapper Too Short.

O.G. Lil Mama,
Candy and Berreta

O.G. Lil Mama.

O.G. Lil Mama, hip-hop artist Honey
& KING THA RAPPER.

O.G. Lil Mama and
Candy Strother DeVore Mitchell.

CHAPTER EIGHT
LENA MOSS

Face of Rap Mothers, Lena Moss is Candy Strother DeVore Mitchell's cousin. Lena's given name is Ilene Moss.

LENA MOSS GREW UP ON THE BEACH, her father was African American; her mother one-half Chinese and one-half Philippine. The youngest of twelve (12) children, Lena was happy as a baby and child. Her mother, referred to as Aunt Rose lived on the beach; she had a lasting effect on Lena, who is a natural beauty.

In her early twenties, Lena met *Superstar Aaron Hall*, the lead singer of *Teddy Riley's* music group, *Guy*. Aaron and Lena soon fell in love after meeting, married and gave birth to a beautiful baby girl they named Kaloni Hall.

Lena and Aaron raised their beautiful daughter on the road while touring the world. As Kaloni grew, she referred to *Superstar Teddy Riley* as her uncle. As the years passed, when not touring with her daddy, Aaron, Kaloni remained at home in Queens with her mother. Today, Kaloni maintains remarkably close bonds with both her mother's, and father's, families.

Currently, Lena Moss is a nurse in New York City. She is a sensitive soul, and a loving-caring nurse, who consistently promotes and markets online commercials from doctors that teach and promote good health practices.

Beautiful Lena Moss.

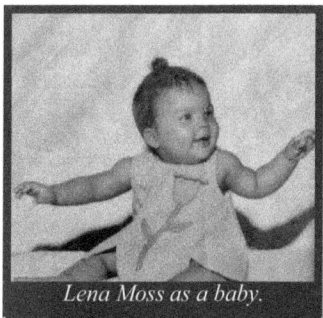

Lena Moss as a baby.

Lena Moss & Kaloni Hall.

Lena Moss & Kaloni Hall.

Lena Moss & Kaloni Hall.

Lena Moss in 2nd Grade.

Lena Moss on her birthday, which is also Halloween!

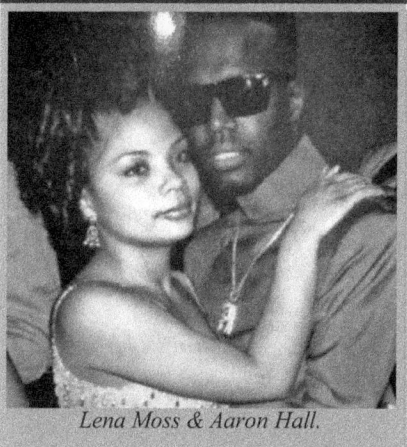

Lena Moss & Aaron Hall.

111

Lena Moss.

Lena Moss & Aaron Hall – 2019.

Aaron and Lena's daughter
Kaloni in grade school.

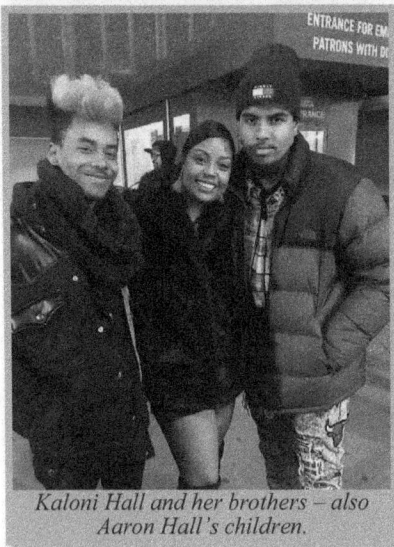
Kaloni Hall and her brothers – also
Aaron Hall's children.

Lena and Kaloni.

Four of Lena Moss's twelve siblings from left to right: Mary Jones, Veronica Moss, Clarence DeVore, and Darryl DeVore with Lena in front.

Lena Moss's mother Aunt Rose.

Lena with her and Aaron Hall's daughter, Kaloni Hall.

Lena and Veronica Moss.

CHAPTER NINE
JAMIE PARIS

Jamie Paris – Mother of JP Cali Smoov of Tha Dogg Pound.

JAMIE WAS RAISED IN A SMALL SUBURBAN TOWN outside of Chicago. Her mother moved Jamie, and sister Michelle, to sunny California to leave blistery winters a thing of the past. Their new home was located in Marina Del Ray, and it was on the beach!

Jamie's mother, a Christian legal secretary, raised her family well. Jamie attends a local church in Venice California currently and carries on the family's traditions.

As a young adult, walking the boardwalk with friends, Jamie found the atmosphere amusing because entertainers and tourists from all over the world were there as well. Her first job was on the boardwalk. Working there she met Tina Marie. They became good friends and took their lunch breaks together. As time progressed, Jamie grew to know the locals who were at the beach daily; many were entertainers. Among them were artists, break-dancers, mimes, roller-skaters, skateboarders, street performers, surfers, and other artists.

When night fell, the local clubs began jamming and as a VIP, Jamie became a *Soul Train* line dancer. She enjoyed some of the best of Los Angeles's mix masters and hung out with the newest and/or most infamous celebrities on *Crenshaw Strip*. Noticed by photographers, producers, and talent agents; Jamie was featured in hit movies such as, *Colors* and *Beat Street*.

Jamie Paris is part Creole, First Nation, and African American. She has an exotic look, which remains unique and *her own*. Her friends, like her, were all unbelievably beautiful – so much so they created a name for themselves . . . *The Rainbow Beauties*. While attending church, Jamie met Michelle Starlot, and they too became good friends and grew closer. Starlet (Michelle's nickname) introduced Jamie to the rich and famous. Jamie dated *Superstars Eddie Murphy* and *Rick James*. *The Rainbow Beauties* were consistently invited to the *Playboy Mansion*. Jamie attended the hottest Hollywood clubs, such as *Carlos & Charlies, Paradise, & Hard Rock Café*. Jamie also dated one of *The DeBarge Group* brothers prior to having a child with *Stevie DeBarge*. She, and *The DeBarge Group* member she had dated prior to Stevie (she will not disclose for personal family reasons), separated on good terms.

Jamie was with *Motley Crue* during their *Home Sweet Home* video and with Janet Jackson when she filmed her, *When I Think of You* video. She also hung out with *Morris Day 7* and traveled on tour with *The DeBarge Group*. She also toured with Latino singer *Selena* and remembers *Selena* as the sweetest, kindest, person you would want to meet.

The DeBarge Show, produced by *Power 106 in LA*, was happening in the era and the DeBarge's treated Jamie like a part of their family. They were remarkably close while *The DeBarge Group* headlined at *Disneyland*. Candy and Jamie went with Starlet and the entire *DeBarge Family* to *Disneyland* and spent a week at the *Disneyland Hotel* while *The DeBarge*

Group performed daily at *Disneyland Hotel* who provided five rooms for their stay. Candy, Starlet and Jamie stayed and had a particularly enjoyable time. They enjoyed *Disneyland* for free, and rode rides, while also attending *The DeBarge Group's* shows and performances.

Apart from *Disney*, members of *The DeBarge Family* would pick Jamie up from school and her classmates were often jealous. Jamie's mother made her break-up with the DeBarge brother she had been dating, and Jamie began hanging with Starlot more often. They spent a lot of time with the richest children and took all expense paid trips through trust funds. The journeys were lavish and included Michelle and Jamie. It was not long until *The DeBarge Group* and their family was back in Jamie's life when *Darrel DeBarge* came to visit and brought bass player *Stevie DeBarge*.

The first time Jamie laid eyes on Stevie was the first time she laid eyes on her future baby's (rapper *JP Cali Smoov*) daddy. Stevie, a famous musician, still plays with *Gerald Albright, The DeBarge Group* and *Stevie Wonder*. It was love at first sight for them both. Stevie got Jamie's number, asked her out for Memorial Day, and after their first date the two of them were smitten. Jamie became pregnant, as time prevailed and Stevie and her married, then moved to Altadena. *The DeBarge Group* brothers, Stevie, and Jamie became roommates. They had a lot of barbeques and parties and at age 27, Steve and Jamie separated. He went on tour and buried himself in his work and she made a fresh start, but Stevie remained a loving and responsible father to their son.

Jamie began working with *BMKY Entertainment Law Firm* – the law firm for the stars. Within one year she became a manager's assistant for A-list actors, directors, musicians, writers, etc. such as *Jim Carey, Samuel Jackson, Kerry Washington, The Wayans's Brothers*, etc.

At age twelve, Jamie's son *West Coast Hip-hop Star JP Cali Smoov* started open mike sessions. He excelled quickly as the most talented and youngest performer, then enrolled in acting classes and landed *Michael Green* as an agent. He has been on *Cartoon Network, Disney Channel*, and *MTV* where they produced a documentary called *JP Cali Smoov American Young Hip-Hop Artist*.

Jamie's son signed with Snoop Dogg's record company *Doggy Style Records* and has toured the world with some of hip-hop's greats, such as

Snoop Dogg, Nipsey Hussle, DJ Quick and more. Jamie is proud of her son's accomplishments.

He was recently awarded a *Certificate of Honor* by United States Congress for work he has done, and is currently doing, helping to guide youth in the right direction. *JP Cali Smoov* tours internationally in support of children causes and starred in a reality television program with *Jermaine Jackson, Jr.*, DeBarge's eldest daughter and starred in short files and pilots. He recently authored his first book, which can be purchased through major online retailer – the title is, *Untold, Unheard of, Unwritten* by John Paul Cali Smoov.

Jamie states, "My family is the greatest gift from God – they are the ultimate love in my life."

Jamie Paris and KING THA RAPPER
at KING'S mom's (Candy Strother DeVore Mitchell's) home.

*Happy family – Jamie Paris, her mother,
JP Cali Smoov and her lovely daughter.*

*Jamie Paris at Tha Dogg Pound
music video set in LA with
KING THA RAPPER.*

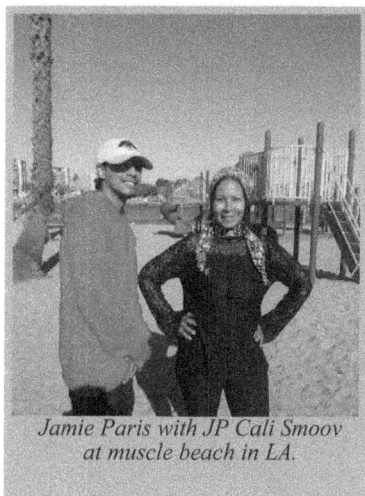

*Jamie Paris with JP Cali Smoov
at muscle beach in LA.*

Jamie Paris is a musician in her own right and is seen here playing the drums.

Jamie Paris and her son, JP Cali Smoov.

JP Cali Smoov on tour.

Jamie Paris and her son, JP Cali Smoov – she remains the most important lady in his life.

Jamie Paris and Stevie DeBarge, post-marriage as life-long friends.

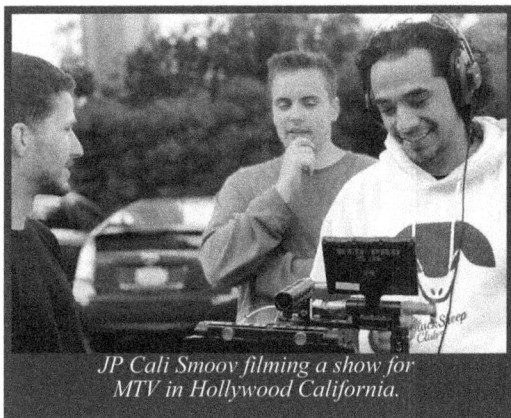

JP Cali Smoov filming a show for MTV in Hollywood California.

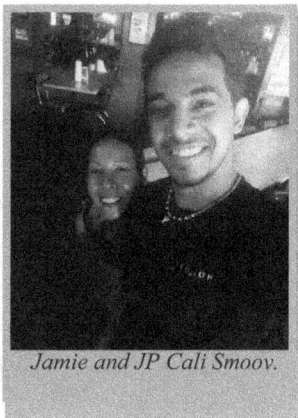

Jamie and JP Cali Smoov.

Jamie Paris and son, West Coast Hip-Hop Star JP Cali Smoov enjoying lunch in the Marina Del Ray Beach – Sunny California!

Jamie Paris, Mark DeBarge, and friends.

*Jamie Paris's son, JP Cali Smoov at age four with his Uncle
James DeBarge helping him. James DeBarge is Superstar El DeBarge's brother.
JP Cali Smoov's daddy is Stevie DeBarge James and El's cousin.*

*The DeBarge Family Group
private home photo – worn with age.*

Superstar EL Debarge on the microphone.

Kristinia DeBarge at four years of age with JP Cali Smoov at three years of age. Kristinia is James DeBarge's daughter and a famous singer.

Jamie Paris as a young adult – private home photo shows her sweet innocent nature.

CHAPTER TEN
NINA WOMACK

GOING VEGAN WITH

NINA

*Nina Womack - entrepreneur wife of
Cecil Womack, son of Mary Wells and Bobby Womack.*

BORN IN LOS ANGELES AS NINA HAIRSTON, this hard-working lady entered the entertainment industry at six (6) years of age when she was discovered in an elevator by a *Dorothy Day Otis / Jack Rose Agency* representative. After signing with them, Nina landed guest roles on television, performed on stage and print modeled for major department store catalogs.

She stopped acting to focus on school during her teenage years and by age eighteen (18) she married her high school sweetheart *Cecil Womack Jr.,* the son of *Mary Wells* (legendary Motown singer) and nephew of *Bobby Womack* (legendary R&B singer).

From youth onward, Miss Hairston's path toward the entertainment industry was benchmarked. After marrying her husband Cecil, she eventually returned to her passion for entertainment. Nina attended *L. A. City College Theater Arcade* before transferring to *Cal State Northridge* where she graduated with honors; since that time, Nina has remained active in entertainment and media.

In September of 1992, Mrs. Womack gave birth to her only child, Dwayne Womack. Albeit everyone refers to Dwayne as *"D"* and he has grown into a successful musician in his own right; also, a producer for some of the music industry's greatest talents, such as: *DJ Quick, Neo, RHIANNA,* & many others.

As the Director of Entertainment for the City of Leimert Park in California, Nina oversees the entertainment for parades that grace the lovely City of Leimert. She also gives free healthy food to the hungry through her, *Let's Be Whole* store that holds a Sunday Giveaway weekly.

As the niece of *Superstar Bobby Womack*, Nina was hired by Superstar Rapper *Ice T*, to manage his California office of *Generation Hip-hop*. She is the Director of *Generation Hip-hop* owned by *Ice T*.

Today, she is either in front of the camera or behind it. When not acting in theater, on television, or in film – Nina is crewing them. She stepped into the producing arena the past several years.

Nina Womack.

Nina Womack as a child.

Nina Womack today.

Nina Womack directed the Martin Luther King event hosted by Leimert Park. In this picture is Candy's lovely daughter West Coast hip-hop artist HONEY with Michael Keith Pop a Disney Actor / child entertainer and Camille Popular who is well-known in Los Angeles as West Coast child hip-hop artist JCM who also appeared on Cartoon Network, Disney Channel, and Nickelodeon.

Nina Womack
Let's Be Whole.

Nina Womack with Nelson Mandela's grandson, Ndaba Thembekile Zweliyajika Mandela.

Nina Womack & DJ Big Boy who is a Hollywood legend presenting hit radio programs for 20+ years.

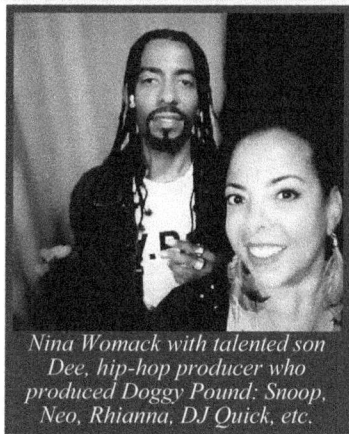

Nina Womack with talented son Dee, hip-hop producer who produced Doggy Pound: Snoop, Neo, Rhianna, DJ Quick, etc.

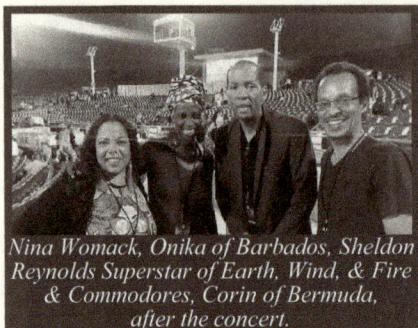

Nina Womack, Onika of Barbados, Sheldon Reynolds Superstar of Earth, Wind, & Fire & Commodores, Corin of Bermuda, after the concert.

Nina Womack & John Salley who is a retired basketball player, talk show host, vegan activist, and wellness entrepreneur.

Nina Womack and her son, Dee.

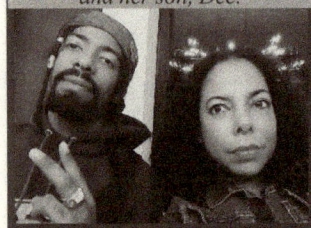

Selfie of Nina, Curtis Young (Dr. Dre's son) & his wife as they strategize how to heal the world through the arts; this power couple is humble and down to help the cause!

Nina Womack in her studio.

Nina Womack & Engineer in the Let's Be Whole studio – getting it right!

Nina Womack.

Left to right, Dee, Nina Womack, Candy Strother DeVore Mitchell, Tina Brown, KING THA RAPPER, West Coast Hip-Hop Artist HONEY and Corey Brown at Leimert Park working on a movie with Superstar Actor& Comedian David Alan Grier.

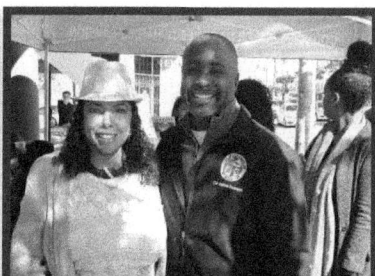

Nina with the awesome Marqueece Harris Dawson Councilman for Los Angeles, CA.

Nina filming, "Let's Be Whole" on the first day of filming, photographed by Candy Strother DeVore Mitchell.

Nina on the set with David Alan Grier.

Nina Womack. Credit: Malco.

Young Nina Womack.

Nina & Candy with friends heading to
Carolos N' Charlie's on Sunset Blvd.
for VIP w/folks such as,
Eddie Murphy, Prince, etc.

Nina playing "Carolina" in Sister Cities
written by Colette Freedman,
at the Stella Adler Theater.

Candy, speaking alongside Nina, on
behalf of her Aunt Ophelia DeVore-
Mitchell at the Martin Luther King
parade in Los Angeles. Ophelia was an
American businesswoman, presidential
advisor, publisher, and model. She
began The Grace Del Marco Agency, a
school about self-development and
modeling where more than 20,000
students including Diahann Carroll,
Cicely Tyson, Gail Fisher,
Susan Taylor, Gil Noble and
Faith Evans attended.

Nina Womack and
Angela Hicks (O.G. Lil Mama).

Nina Womack poolside.

Nina produced Tha Dogg Pound's
KING THA RAPPER music video, "Rollin."

Candy's eldest son Ricardo with an infamous doctor preparing for the, "Let's Be Whole Show," at Nina's studio.

Nina Womack and Candy Strother DeVore Mitchell on the "Let's Be Whole Show."

Filming Nina Womack's, "Let's Be Whole Show."

Filming Nina Womack's, "Let's Be Whole Show."

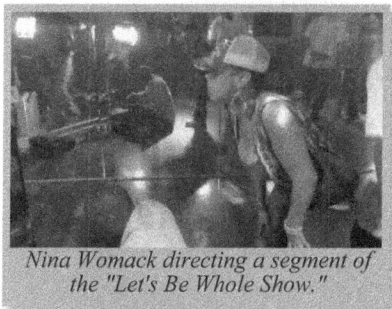

Nina Womack directing a segment of the "Let's Be Whole Show."

Nina Womack in, "Murder at Thick City."

Nina Womack in, "Murder at Thick City."

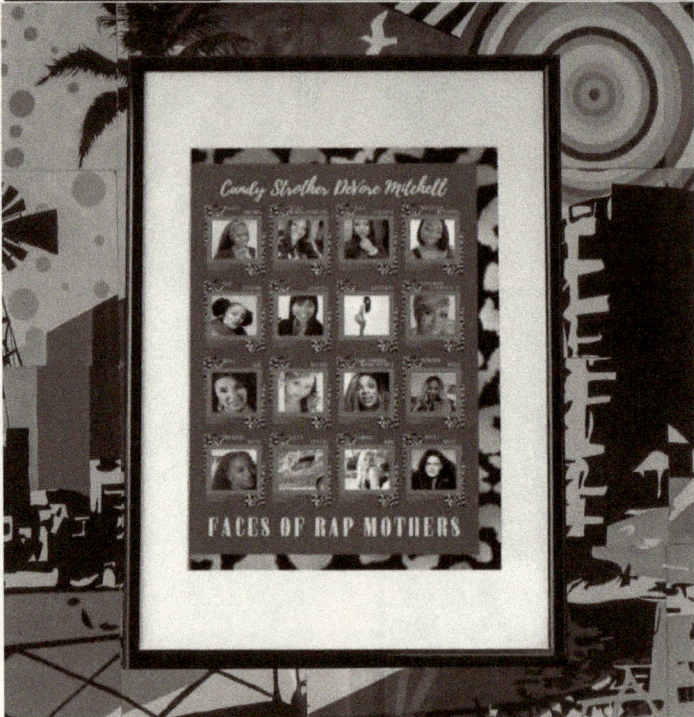

CHAPTER ELEVEN
SHARON LYNETTE YOUNG

What Does God Want for My Life?

Sharon Lynette Young (Berreta) from Troy New York.

BORN ON 6 NOVEMBER 1963. my parents, Margaret Ann, and Joseph Leon Walker, had four (4) additional children. I am their eldest daughter. The eldest of my siblings is Anastacia, my brother. Followed by me, is my first younger sister Donna Marie, and our youngest brother Wrayuntwon. My mother had an additional four (4) children before meeting my father; the eldest to youngest are Myrtis Louise Price, Landress Larue Buckley, Anthony Lamar Buckley, and Kim Renee Buckley.

Currently, I reside in Los Angeles and surprisingly enough, I have four (4) children of my own. Aurelia Lakee Woodgett is forty (40), Ricky Darnell Walker is thirty-five (35), Indica Laree Walker is thirty-two (32) and Channerik Anthony Lloyd Walker is twenty-nine (29). I have also been blessed with six (6) grandchildren Jaicen Darnell Walker is fourteen (14), Jaiden is twelve (12), Kayli is six (6) – they are my son Ricky's children. Ricky has two baby mommas "both Christinas." One is Christina Maria and, the other, is Christina Drake.

Indica has a son Gesa Anthony Ngenwena, and her husband is Gesa Thomas Ngenwena. Aurelia has not given me any grandchildren yet – maybe soon. Channerik has two children, and two stepchildren, their names are Daylen Stefon Lopez - is five (5), Channerik Anthony Lloyd Walker Jr. - is one (1); Channerik's stepsons Paten Dixon - is twelve (12) and Joshua Emmanuel - is six (6). Channerik also has two baby mommas - Kimberly Dixon and Madie Lopez – with a new baby on the way with Kimberly.

Eric Charles Berry (aka *Bobby Drakenit*) is my husband of eleven (11) years and is my true soulmate. He has two beautiful daughters. The eldest Diamond – is twenty-two (22) and youngest Destiny Jamiah – is eleven (11).

Eric and I own a recording studio. *Off the Planet Productions*. It is located in North Hollywood. Our business has been in existence for about five (5) years. We are blessed to have renowned artists record music in our studio, of which I am enormously proud. We took a chance, and it has resulted in distinguished artists collaborating with us.

Off the Planet Productions has also experienced great producers as well, such as *Focus* who is *Eminem* and *Dr. Dre's* producer. *Focus* came to produce a song for *Omar Gooding* aka *Big O*. We have had *Omar Gooding* in our studio, and the entire *Moe-Doe Family*. Our own children have recorded hit songs in the studio; their songs never really made it big - big, but they have had limited success and are all hit records. If someone knows music and has opportunity to hear their work - they really get behind them and what we are doing. We have our own television shows, Bobby began *Ice Cream Caken'it TV*; and my girl *Candy Strother Devore Mitchell* and I have started a reality show, *Face of Rap Mothers*.

We are building an Internet promotion platform utilizing music and videos. Also, have developed a few clothing lines, 1) *Off the Planet*, 2) *Living in London*, and 3) *Ice Cream and Caken'it* clothing. The products are qualitative and attractive, and our shoes are chill.

Vamos-Por La Estrella is registered with *ASCAP Publishing Company*. It was created for the *2018 World Cup* in our studio by *Shawndale Mackey* aka *Pressplay* for the Mexican teen for the *World Cup*.

I have moved around out here in California, and worked with many actors, rappers, singers and people in general. Some of the folks I have met, worked with, and consider friends or family include *Flex Alexander, David*

A. Arnold, Honey and John Blunt, Tamar Braxton, Chris Brown, Tina Brown, Affion Crockett, Monica Davis, OG DUV MAC DOGG, Snoop Dogg, Mike Epps, Vivica Fox, Omar Gooding, Angela Gilchrist Guyton, Arsenio Hall, Tyaunna Harris, Angela Hicks, Romeo Holloway, Ice T, Igor Beats, Janet Jackson, Michael Jackson, Rick James, Jelly Roll, Sir Jenks, Magic Johnson, Tina Marie, Alonzo Marks, Candy Strother DeVore-Mitchell, Charlie Murphy, Eddie Murphy, Nicole Murphy, Jamie Paris, Tashan Pierce, Eric. B and Rakim, Smokey Robinson, Tony Rock, Sharvar Ross, John Salley, Tupac Shakur, Todd Sims one of the greatest dance choreographers he has worked with Usher, Jamika Lawson Smith, Chris Spencer, Tha Dogg Pound, The DeBarge Family, The Gap Band, The New Edition, The Wayans Brother's (Damon, Keenan, Marlin and Shawn), Mike Tyson, Kim Whitley, Shanice Wilson, Nina Womack, Stevie Wonder, Xzibit, Yero, and so many more – there are too many to mention.

Additionally, I have worked on many movie sets, such as *Baby Boom Real Estate Stories, Beauty Shop* play, *Coming to America, Eastsiders, Raising Whitley* and *BET Awards Short Films*, Theater Awards, and again too many to mention.

Of course, I have experienced good and tough times in Los Angeles. I have gone from being homeless without food to eat and not knowing how to make it out of those situations, to where we are today. I was homeless for four (4) years with no consistent food to eat, but I smiled, while all I wanted to do was die. Folks going through a situation like that hide it from everyone, especially people they love and care about, so they are not judged wrongly. I stayed prayered up, and remained positive, while working hard at what I believe in. You know you strive to be the best person you can, and then, find out who God wants you to be, and learn what the Creator wants from you. Every day now, I thank God for getting me through those times.

Faith is what helps make a success in this world, but not faith alone, you must combine it with focus and demanding work. You must keep from allowing things happening around you, good or bad, to stop your grind. I know God has seen me through all the experiences I have surpassed and brought me to the better side of the matter in the end.

While I may not have all the things in life I covet – I know if I keep my faith in the *Most High,* he will give me my heart's desire. Ask, believe, and work hard; you will receive it. Faith in God's timing, not your own, while giving love to people, returns it to you in the end. What I came to know is, if you keep positive people around you - people who are successful – you will become successful. Experts say the top five (5) people in your life tell the story of your life's experiences. If you surround yourself with negative broken people - negative and broken will be your life experience. Pay attention to the people who are making it. Observe what they do, and how they move, and you will understand what I am saying. You must educate yourself. Not just through studies of books; also, through studies of people. I have learned a lot since childhood, to be a teenager, to becoming a full-grown-woman. Travels from New York City to Detroit to Hollywood resulted in a lot of life lessons for me. So, trust yourself to improve and have faith in God – then watch it happen for you.

My mother and father met in Little Rock Arkansas, where they both were born. My mother's mother was Aubrey Adams, and my mother's father, Jimmy Alcorn. My mother has a sister, Louise Jackson. Mom and Louise grew up together in Little Rock. They went to school together and hung out until they both were married, had children, and moved away to start their families in various parts of the world.

When my mother met my father, she had had four (4) children already from a previous relationship as a I stated earlier. My Aunt Jerry thought my mother was incredibly beautiful and introduced her to her brother who, of course, is my dad, Mr. Joseph Leon Walker. Upon meeting, they fell in love and married; that is how my parents met. They lived in Little Rock after marrying. for about a year. and had my brother Anastacia there. Afterward, they relocated to Troy. My father had family there, his brother, my Uncle Buster and Aunt Flossy with their children and other family members nearby. While my folks resided there, I was born, and later my sister Donna. We were born in Lemer Hospital. This is life began and my very first memories are derived from there. It was great when we were children. I learned a lot of shit as a kid, things kids should not see or know at an early age when innocent – but you live and learn as they say. Most children experience these sorts of events growing up because older cousins, brothers, or sisters, tend to younger siblings the wrong things and sometimes adults do crazy shit around children too. Of course, you were not allowed to say anything, or you would be in big trouble; so, we took it all in and went with the flow. When you are a child, you cannot do anything about life around you for the most part. What life brings you – you endure - you keep your head down, spirits high, eyes on heaven to muster through it all.

Troy was a ridiculously small town, and everybody knew one another. With a lot of family – like we had in Troy – everyone kind of knew what we were up to. In that way, a small town *can be* beneficial.

My father was a roofer. He also hustled pool and dice to make extra income. Mother worked for *RPI College* in the cafeteria as the cashier; of course, she was also a housewife and took care of us children. My mother was beautiful, with a great body, and could cook her ass off. What I remember most about Troy was when my mother and father took us to the park, and we had barbeque. All our family – cousins, aunts, uncles, and others came, it was cool to have many family members together. My mother loved to dress us up. For us girls, she spared no expense in getting our party dresses and hair done. She put us in beauty pageants – Stacy and I were entered in *The King and Queen Contest* at Prospect Park. We did not win because my brother Stacy started clowning around. He kept talking while we were to walk in a circle with our hands at our sides without talking while looking straight ahead. Due to his shenanigans, we came in 2nd place. It was a wonderful experience though. My mother did this a lot and taught us to want something more in life.

Mom entered Donna in the *Miss Troy Boy's Club (Miss T.B.C.) Contest*. Donna won. She was beautiful. She rode in the parade down Federal Street where people were lined up on both sides of waving at her. She was in my father's convertible. She was sitting in the passenger's seat while the first and second place winners sat in the backseat waving. Our family members walked alongside the convertible - we were so happy Donna won. My mother had Donna's hair on point, and she wore a stunning dress, there was no other choice but for her to win. Through our mother's efforts, we were always winning something. Mom liked to keep us girls dressed like little dolls while she kept us as busy as best, she could. Our mom made certain our home was clean and well-decorated. It was very beautiful - you could eat off the floor if you were so inclined – she kept it that clean.

In Troy, our home was on 9th and Federal Streets. Aunt Jerry and Uncle Bill stayed up the hill from us. Uncle Buster and Aunt Flossy stayed on 8th Street. We grew up with their kids . . . these are my cousins Beverly, Billy Jean, Clem, Kenny, Marvin, Mickey, Net, Peter, Phillis, Roxanne, Shed, Tina, and Wayne.

Billy Jean, Donna, Stacy, Tina, and I were in school together because of our ages, but Donna, Stacy and I were closest in age and ran all over Troy and Albany together. We enjoyed hanging out at the bowling alley a lot. Stacy used to take us to the Hudson River too. I recollect my mom was always worried we would fall in the river and drown. The river was dangerous and if you fell in it, was a grave issue. Lots of folks were not found when they fell in, but we loved to go there and hang out anyway.

Our home was a three-bedroom apartment in a four-unit building design, with two apartments upstairs, and two downstairs. Ours was upstairs on the left. My Aunt Ruth and Uncle Floyd were on the right of us. My Aunt Willie Mae lived downstairs under Aunt Ruth. A neighbor by the name of, Mr. Strickland was there and another door across the hall from him was to the very scary basement.

Walking up the stairs you turned left, and our door was on right. We walked into the living room upon entering the apartment. Mom and dad's room was on the left. Another small room was where Donna and I slept.

137

On the right of the living room, was our kitchen and another bedroom where Stacy slept. When you walked into the kitchen there was a backdoor and porch – like Lucy and Ricky Ricardo's apartment in the *I Love Lucy* show. Our porches were connected, and our building was the only building on our street, other than a black house on the corner of the block. There was a nice old white lady who lived in that house. We feared her at first. Her home looked kind of spooky, but the lady would come out and talk with us, she made us peanut butter and jelly crackers. She appeared alone and was sweet to us. We had never had peanut butter and jelly crackers before. Today, I still love them, and they are a favorite snack now.

To the left of our apartment building were green stairs to *RPI College* where my mother worked. We would hang out in the dorms and on campus frequently. Our favorite park was Prospect Park. A big swimming pool was located there. I remember being at the pool or park on holidays. One time, a fight broke out between my mom and dad, and we had to leave early because mom was angry with dad. My father knew my mother could not swim and he had picked her up and threw her in the deep end of the pool. She was so mad she could have killed him (not literally – just as an expression). We did not really realize what had happened at our ages – we tried to get her to stay – but the party was over. I have always felt my father made a poor decision that day. I do not think he thought about what he was doing or that it would get the reaction it did from my mom.

When our folks were at work, like most children, we were everywhere – we had a babysitter - Fat Baby, which is what all the kids called her. After school, we went to her house. She had set us on the floor on newspapers to feed us and then let us go outside and play until mom returned from work. Usually, we went to Tina and Billy Jean's house because they lived right near Fat Baby's. From there, we were all over Troy as cousins having fun, and we got into all sorts of trouble. One time, I recollect my sister Donna, my brother Stacy and I going to Holiday Inn at the bottom of the hill downtown Troy, where we played in the rooms when people left.

We were so young. That was crazy. Stacy began taking maids' tips. One time a maid found him, and we were busted. The police were called. We were petrified because we knew if the police came, we would get our asses beat. We realized we had to find a way out of the room. There was another door on the other side of the room, connected to the room we were in, and thankfully, Stacy got the door open. We escaped through that room and slipped out of the hotel. Afterward, we ran so fast we had to run up dirt hills and then we just kept running. Stacy found a big hole in the hill and said, "Lets hide in here so we can get some rest in case they are looking for us." We waited about an hour, looked out, did not see anyone, and continued back to Fat Baby's house before mom picked us up. The funny thing about all of this was, we were only four, five, and six years old with Stacy being oldest. Back in those days' kids hung out, and folks did not appear to worry if you got home on time and did not get into trouble. Mom and dad taught us not to talk to strangers, never to trust people we did not know, and not to go anywhere with strangers, which we listened to.

About five (5) years ago, I went back to Troy to chill with my family and it was as if I went back in time to the 60's – like I had never left. Everything looked the same. The building we lived in was gone. The green stairs were not green anymore. The lady in the house on the left was gone. Other than that, it was about the same and for the most part it was great being back home. This is not the first time I have gone back home – I went for my father's and Uncle Buster's funerals but only stayed a few days. Over the years, we have not gotten to have the same bonding time as years ago though.

Back in the early days, when family and friends got together on the weekend and threw block parties where cooking food outside was the norm – a DJ would spin, and the fire department would turn the fire hydrant on its highest for us so we could run through the water. It was memorable. Our block parties started at about six or seven in the evening and lasted sometimes until two or three in the morning. Today, they have block parties, but they are held at someone's home. I miss the family love and unity we had in Troy – it was a good era.

After living in big cities – Troy is too slow paced for me now. I would not know what to do with myself for a lengthy time living there. All the family love might be what I need because I was incredibly happy when I was with my family, I had not seen in over fifteen (15) years. They were the same loving and kind people I remembered. Still kicking back together, celebrating birthdays, holidays, etc. I miss family and would enjoy staying in touch more on social media through Facebook, iPhone, etc. We do Facetime – it is not the same as being there though. Family is supposed to be everything.

The first time our mother took us to church, it was down the hill from our home. It was one of the scariest times in my life. My mother was called to the front of the alter. Next thing I knew, she was crying and rolling all over the floor with white stuff coming out of her mouth. I had no idea what was going on. It was scary. My sister Donna and I never wanted to go back to church again after that. We believed something evil was happening to her. To this day, I would like to know what was going on with her. Since I have grown up, I have visited churches and studied with Jehovah Witnesses and the Hebrew Israelites. I read the Bible for Myself with the *Most High* guiding me, which gave me a true understanding of his word and what he expects from me. This means I am to keep all six hundred and ninety commandments if I want to live the good life.

Since my mother had four (4) children before she married my father, we did not have an opportunity to know our oldest sister Myrtis Louise Price until she came to live with us. She was born in Chicago. Until age twelve (12) she lived with her father who was Odell Price. It was exciting to meet Myrtis because we did not know we had an older sister. She was very pretty and helped at home. She was happy to live with us and our mother. Soon after Myrtis came to live with us, our big brother Landress Larue Buckley came to live with us. Now, Landress was a crazy big brother who was into boxing at an early age. He was a great fighter and won most of his boxing matches. He was also a hustler and, he was mean when we first met him. As he aged, he grew softer, and we started to love him – I am proud to call him my brother now.

Overall – growing up was a blessing for me. We were tight. I learn-ed how to treat all people I meet equally and, on a level playing field no matter their station in life because I know life can be a rollercoaster at times and as I stated earlier, "You watch and learn." Once you have done that you have a good idea of what is what and who is who and that good people come from all walks of life.

I hope you enjoy my images that follow. Many are from the cellphone, others are dated and not well preserved, but they are real times with real people that I am thankful to know in this life.

More to come in upcoming editions of, *Faces of Rap Mothers*.

*Berreta with Eddie Murphy and Johnny Gill
lead singer of world-famous music group The New Edition
and below with infamous Actress Vivid Fox.*

Berreta and husband, West Coast hip-hop entertainer & radio talk show host, MC Bobby Drakenit.

Berreta and husband, West Coast hip-hop entertainer & radio talk show host, MC Bobby Drakenit.

Berreta and husband Eric Berry aka MC Bobby Drakenit.

*Off the Planet
Berreta and Bobby Drakenit.*

Berreta and Bobby Drakenit new clothing line introductions.

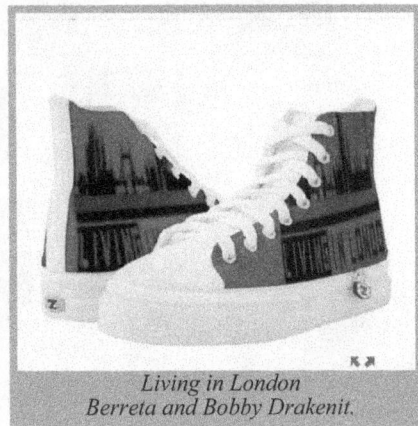

*Living in London
Berreta and Bobby Drakenit.*

143

Berreta's son, Anthony – Hip-Hop Artist Channerik.

Sharon Lynette Young "Berreta" with her son, Anthony. "Channerik."

Berreta's husband in their studio, "Off the Planet."

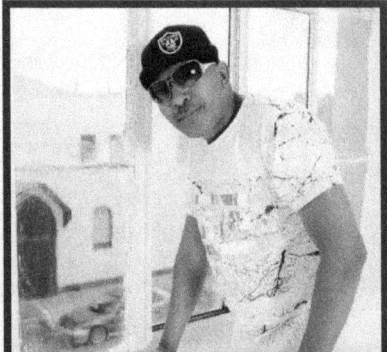

P.M.C. Bobby Dragenit, Berreta's man.

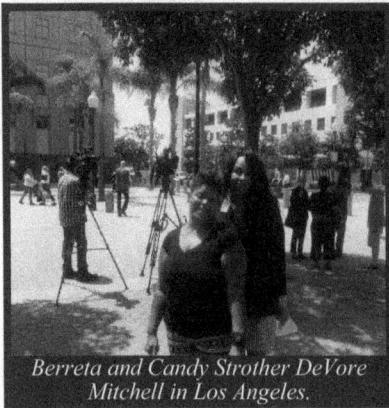

Berreta and Candy Strother DeVore Mitchell in Los Angeles.

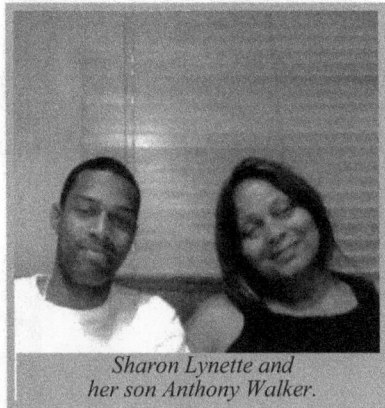

Sharon Lynette and her son Anthony Walker.

Berreta and Performers.

Berreta and Snoop Dogg.

Sharon Lynette Young's children and grandchildren.

*Berreta (middle),
Val Young and Shari Headley.*

Berreta and Xzibit.

Berreta and Xzibit.

Berreta in Production.

Berreta and Ja'Net DuBois.

Berreta and Tracee Ellis Ross.

Berreta and friend.

Berreta and
Shanice Wilson.

Berreta and KURUPT of the Dogg
Pound, OG Lil Mama, Candy, KING
THA RAPPER, Lawrence Lee Valle,
and a friend at Off the Planet.

Berreta.

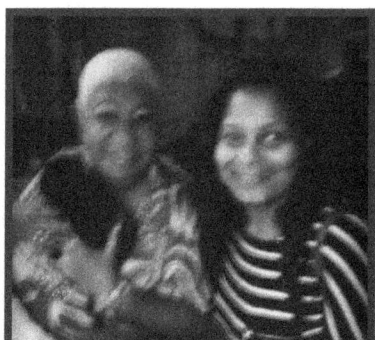

Berreta and Actress
Comedian Luenell.

Berreta, Singer Shanice
Wilson and friend.

147

*Berreta and
Shanice Wilson.*

*Berreta and
Bern Nadette Stanis.*

Berreta and Shanice Wilson.

Berreta and Eddie Murphy.

Berreta and Ice Cube.

Berreta and Eddie Murphy.

Berreta and Keith Sweat.

Berreta, Keith Sweat and their friend.

KING THA RAPPER and M.C. Bobby Dragenit.

Berreta and Ralph Tresvant.

Berreta at Snoop's Book Signing.

Berreta and KING THA RAPPER, McKinley Ave, and Roscoe.

149

Berreta and Shari Headley.

Berreta, KURUPT, Candy, Timbo, KING THA RAPPER, Honey, and Lawrence Lee.

Berreta at event.

Berreta, M.C. Bobby Dragenit and friend.

Berreta.

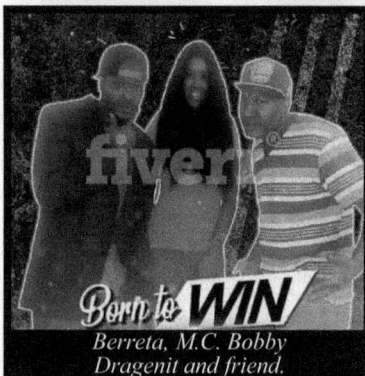
Berreta, M.C. Bobby Dragenit and friend.

Berreta and friend.

Berreta's son.

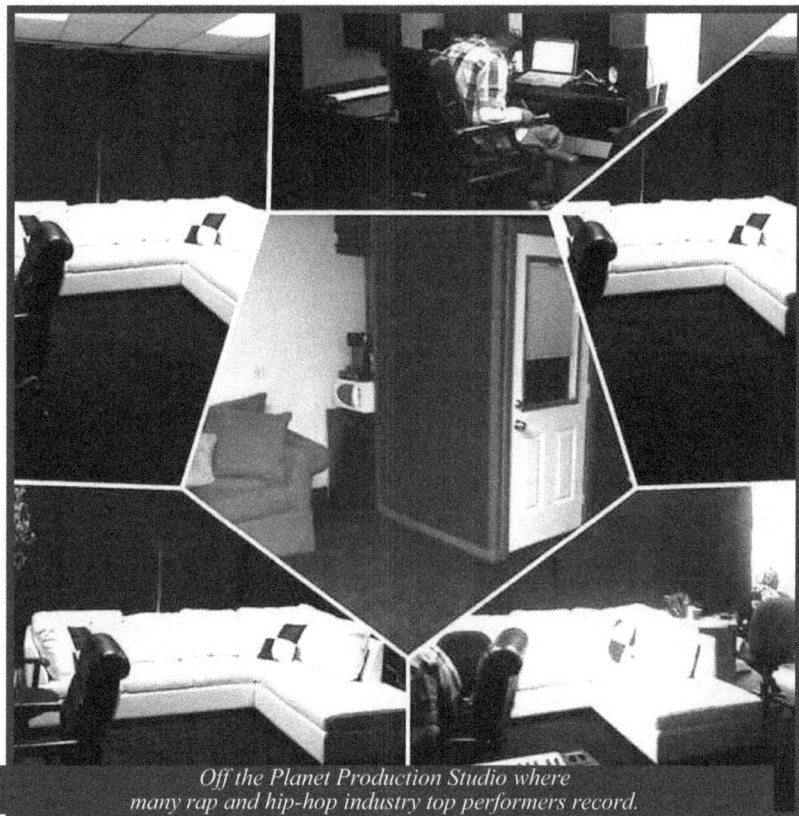

Off the Planet Production Studio where many rap and hip-hop industry top performers record.

Berreta on Mainstreet Billboard.

Berreta on Mainstreet Billboard.

IN RECOGNITION #1
OG DUV MAC DOGG

James Woodard is the Executive Producer of Face of Rap Mothers and known as OG DUV MAC DOGG. He is here with Snoop Dogg on his left, and Candy Strother DeVore Mitchell on his right.

JAMES DAVID (KADONIA) WOODARD JR. born 19 October 1971 in Long Beach, California, started his career age twelve (12) when he fell in love with music. His father played guitar leisurely, and in church. His cousin, *Ran Dogg* practiced the drums in his family's garage, and played every Sunday in church. James hung out on stage with his father's group, *Danny, and the Boys*, during parties and at night clubs. *Ran Dogg* continued to become one of the producers for *Tha Dogg Pound*; and is known for *Daz* and *The Low Life's*.

While attending *Millikan High School*, OG DUV MAC became friends with Anthony Lee (*DJ Quiet One*), who was fierce on mixing and scratching. Woodard and *DJ Quiet* were the dynamic duo at house parties. OG rapped to *DJ Quiet's* mixes and as time progressed, *DJ Quiet* coached James to scratch and mix as he developed interests for it, which is where he realized he was much more than a rapper. Not long afterward, Woodard became known as *DJ Moo* or *Shamoo*. He began rapping and earning his DJ experience and held long-term collaboration with rapper Johnny Fitzgerald Askew, who performed under the name of *Pookie Loc* aka *Fra Du Roc*. As a teenager, *OG Duv Mac Dogg* joined with *G-Celly Cell* and was featured on *Nationwide Rip Ridaz II*. Additionally, he was friends with Shawn Ivy, Warren Griffin III, and Calvin Cordozar Broadus, later known as *Domino, Warren G,* and *Snoop Dogg*.

After spending a few years in LA, Gardenia, and Compton, James' family moved back to LBC, and he met *Pookie Loc* where he reconnected with Cousin Michael Tubbs who led him to a young lady that led him to *DJ Chilly Chill* from *Da Lench Mob*. At that point is where *OG Duv Mac Dogg* states his career in rap really started. When Woodard and *DJ Chilly Chill* met, *OG DUV MAC* submitted material and *Chill* collaborated with him right away.

Da Curb Cyde auditioned for *Tamika* at *Ruthless Records* and was signed by *DJ Unique* at *King Pin Records/EMI*. Woodard was a producer and member of *Bone-Thugs & Harmony* before signing with King Pin and changed his name from *DJ Moo* to *Duv Mac* because his focus changed to M.C.

At the end of the contract with *King Pin, Da Curb Cyde* parted and created young *Curb Cyde*, who is still under *Chilly Chill Ent*. After *Da Curb Cyde* parted, *DUV MAC* turned over a new leaf in his career and began writing, producing, and performing *Gangsta Gospel Hip-hop*, he signed a record deal with *G-Like Music Group* featuring the *Stella* award-winning group *SYG's 4/C* (for Christ). He also joined artists such as *AKG, BigTone, Bur Rabbis,* and *Low Key*.

Over time, *OG DUV MAC* has kept pace, built skills, and developed the ammunition to establish his companies. One of them is *Faultline Productionz*, which is a grass roots endeavor he began at his dining room table – upgraded to his garage – eventually becoming a mobile endeavor to reach artists through studios on the go. *Team Faultline Records* represents new artists, such as (listed alphabetically) *Bugsy, Da Bloc, E Brock, Fella Brown* and *Two Hollows and a Pistol*. While *OG DUV MAC* has a private recording studio in Moreno Valley conceived and developed with modern technology – *Faultline Productionz* moves mobility in meeting artists' needs with picking tracks and recording songs mastered at *Kadonia's Music Studios* without having to commit to a brick n' mortar experience.

OG DUV MAC's concept results in an infinite number of buildings for studio recordings and postproduction resulting in the *Get The Song Done* model where starts can rise on the go anywhere, anytime, anyway. His production style coupled with caring for his artists is helping continue the *Inland Empire* music community that has spawned the likes of *J Roc Records and Ent.* in Atlanta Georgia and *The Fluu* in NJ.

Compilation albums:
- *After Shock 7.2*

- *Dead End*
- *Drunk in the Spirit*
- *Nationwide Rip Ridaz II*
- *Welcome to the Bricks*

Discography:
- 1997: *Nationwide Rip Ridaz II*

Singles:
- *How Ya'll Gone Steal My Swag*
- *Kadonia Get It Done*
- *Microphone Fiend*
- *Stop Da Beefin*

Studio albums:
- 2005: *Let It Flow*
- 2006: *Drunk in the Spirit*
- 2007: *After Shock 7.2*
- 2008: *Dead End*
- 2010: *Welcome to the Bricks*

References:
- *DaBloc at Last.fm*
- *DaBloc Blog*
- *DaBloc on Twitter*
- *DaBloc951 channel at YouTube*
- *Duv Mac aka at MySpace*
- *Kadonia*
- *Kadonia at iLike*
- *Kadonia at Yahoo! Music*
- *Official S*

OG DUV MAC DOGG and his cousin Snoop Dogg.
also, KING THA RAPPER'S sister HONEY (also a rap artist) and
Sharon Lynette Young better known as Berreta.

From left to right, Snoop Dogg, OG DUV MAC DOGG and friend.

OG DUV MAC DOGG on Detroit Unplugged.

DUV MAC DOGG, KING THA RAPPER mom
Candy Strother DeVore Mitchell and JP Cali Smoov mom Jamie Paris.

157

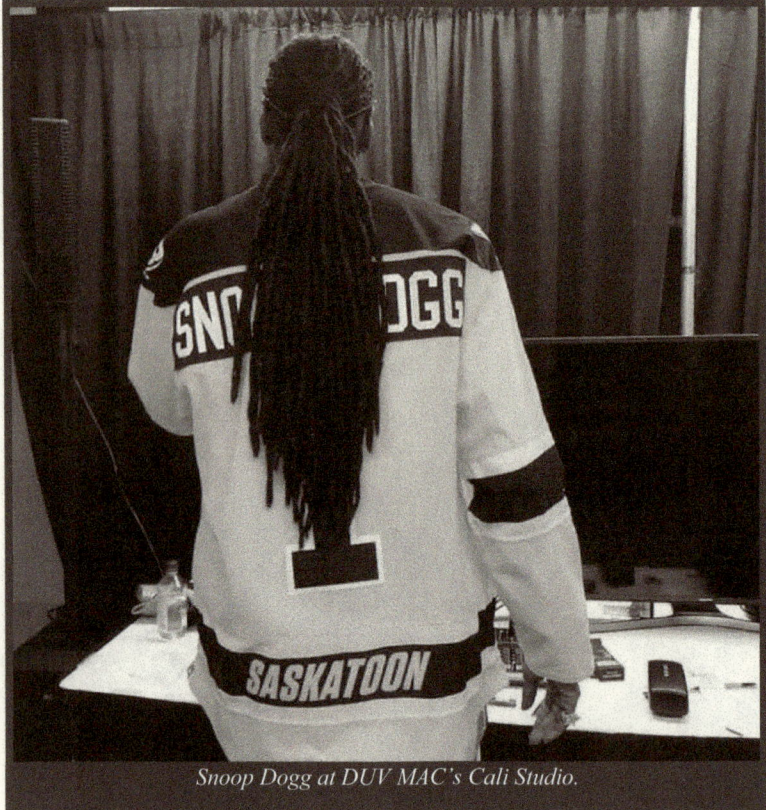

Snoop Dogg at DUV MAC's Cali Studio.

IN RECOGNITION #2
MINISTER JAMIKA LOVE WISDOM

I can do all things through Christ which strengthened me. (KJV), Philippians 4.13.

~Minister Jamika Love Wisdom

Jamika Lawson Smith
Minister Jamika Love Wisdom.

I AM A GOD-FEARING WOMAN depending on *His Grace and Mercy* for everything in my life! I was born an identical twin and my mother also gave birth to one other child, which is my brother John.

I grew up in LA, and attended *Western Avenue Elementary*, John *Muir Junior High* and *Manual Arts High School*. During the 70's and 80's -

gangs were taking off and drugs ravished our city - giving us the blues. I lost many young friends to gang violence and saw many of my family members suffer from the effects of crack. Growing up around so much dysfunction, I ended up having two teenage pregnancies at age sixteen (16) and seventeen (17) years. Since I needed money, when my children's father was not employed, I turned to the streets for extra cash and managed to escape hard drugs but tried to make extra money from time-to-time hustling. I was not good at dealing drugs - so I pursued life as a hairstylist, which is where I found my gift for ministering.

Encouraging others is where I most often found myself. Helping folks through a tough time was where I shined. Even though I had had my own life struggles and had to encourage myself with positive thoughts and in listening to my grandmother and Godmother Dee, my customers returned to partake of my caring heart in addition to the quality of stylist work I provided. I continued working on hair and connected to cool people who helped me add to my inherent capabilities.

A man's gift maketh room for him, and
bringeth him before great men, Proverbs 16:13.

Later, I moved to Las Vegas, Nevada and joined a ministry that provided training in becoming an ordained Minister under leadership Willie J. Frink at *Rose of Sharon Faith Ministry*. I had many duties in the church from teaching, and prayer service to ushering. I decided to get a ministry education; so, I went to *Liberty University* and *Grace Christian University* for five (5) years where I earned certificates in *Christian Counseling*. Today, I am married to a wonderful man, my husband, Mr. Al Smith (Bishop). We have eleven (11) children between us from previous relationships, and one child together, our son, King Smith.

"Wise Words of Encouragement."

From time to time, we are faced with challenges whether with our children, spouses, jobs, schools, etc.; it is best for these challenges to approach them as learning experiences for elevation. Life is always teaching us; always willing to expand us, to become a better us. It is solely up to our understanding with the situation if will have to repeat the lesson or elevate to the next level of learning.

No one has arrived at the place of complete fulfillment spiritually and knowledgably. The good Lord made it that way to keep us humble as well as to keep us in a place where we will seek Him for answers. This is a way to build a person relationship with prayer.

If you consider yourself to be a *Child of God*, then go to Him in the morning, preferably when you rise, and supplicate in prayer. It does not take long and drawn-out efforts, just simply say. . .

Lord, as I go throughout my day, open my
understanding, and cause me to receive the wisdom in

the lesson that the universe will send me for peace and elevation.

Thank you, father for loving and sending your son to die for my sins, I am grateful.

You see, when we keep ourselves in a place of humility and leave ourselves open to receive God's blessings in the day – we are blessed. Remember, it is always Love because God is Love! Have a blessed and prosperous day loved ones.

Beloved, let us love one another: for love is of God; and everyone that loveth is born of God, and knoweth God, 1 John 4.7.

~Minister Jamika (Jazz) "Jamika Love Wisdom"

Minister Jamika Love Wisdom.

Jamika and Tamika.

ABOUT THE AUTHOR
CANDY STROTHER DEVORE MITCHELL

CANDY STROTHER DEVORE MITCHELL'S aunt was a civil rights leader who worked alongside *Dr. Martin Luther King.* This resulted in Candy's understanding, and interest, in human rights activism. Eventually, she aired in national news broadcasts and testified on Capitol Hill concerning topics that aid children and families.

Apart from her civil and human right pursuits, Candy is an actress, author, mom, and executive producer of *The Face of Rap Mothers Show,* which, like her book series, is comprised of rap and hip-hop mothers, sisters, aunts, cousins, etc. working to build better futures through entrepreneurial and solopreneur efforts. She is also CEO of *Black Cash Universal Studios Entertainment* and two of her children are rap and hip-hop artists, namely *Honey* and *KING THA RAPPER.*

Currently, Candy resides in Los Angeles, some of her children reside with her and her husband. Her next book release is December 2019.

JUST A FYI: the next volume in the *Faces of Rap Mothers* series includes remarkably interesting Rap Mothers such as, Laurice Adams, Antoinette Ames, Dianna Boss, Carlene Corsey, Tiffani Lewis, Rolanda Shoulders Macharia, Fedra Thompson, and Bonnie Williams, among others.

Make certain to join the Faces of Rap Mothers mailing roster for a list of events / locations for book signings and special promotions, visit https://www.donnaink.net or https://www.facesofrapmothers.com. Write contact@donnainkpublications.com for more information.

Candy Strother DeVore Mitchell – Author.

VISIT THE AUTHOR
WEBSITE | SOCIAL MEDIA

FACES OF RAP MOTHERS Website
https://www.facesofrapmothers.com

Beat Deep Books | DonnaInk Publications Website
https://www.donnaink.net (For deep pocket discounts!)

Facebook Fan Page
https://www.facebook.com/facesofrapmothers

Instagram
https://www.instagram.com/facesofrapmothers

Pinterest
https://www.pinterest.com/facesofrapmothers

Twitter
https://www.twitter.com/facesofrapmothers

YouTube
https://www.youtube.com/facesofrapmothers

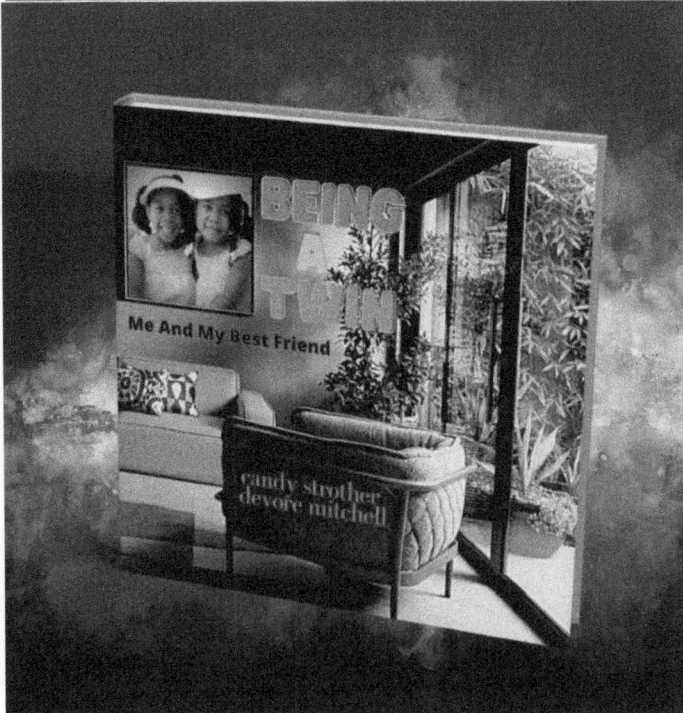

ABOUT THE PUBLISHER
DONNAINK PUBLICATIONS, L.L.C.

No Other Ink Will Do!
It's a Donna Ink for You!

Your Story

DONNAINK PUBLICATIONS, L.L.C.

PUBLISHER & WRITER SUPPORT SERVICER

Woman-owned small publishing house featuring over forty eclectic authors from nine countries and five continents delivering works discriminating readers love, with organic growth verticals coupled with inherent drive for quality productions both readers and writers love. We also extend a suite of services support, such as author representation, book development, cover design, editorial, ghostwriting, layout & design, marketing, press kits, public relations, reviews, website content & design, etc.

PUBLISHER OF:

FACES OF RAP MOTHERS
RAP MOTHERS SAVE THE DAY!

DONNAINK PUBLICATIONS, L.L.C. GENRE IMPRINTS

Ms. Donna L. Quesinberry, Founder & President of DonnaInk Publications, is an author, brand & business development guru, desktop publisher, editor, entrepreneur, ghostwriter, management consultant, presentation expert, press & public relations analyst, and much more. Donna, often referred to as "Q", aids her authors & clients with burgeoning market presence while developing their work(s) & image to gain recognition from readers and industry alike. Her authors have risen from novice to award-winning publications, reality television, screenplay, speaking engagements, Ted Talks, etc. Donna is a recognized author & poet in her own right and a mother of five adult children. She currently resides in the Town of Carthage, snuggled in the Sandhills of North Carolina, where she manages a National Historic Registry Airbnb with traumatic brain injury (TBI) survivor son Jamie Hatcher.

Author Representation | Book Development | **Cover Design** | Editorial | **Ghostwriting**
Layout & Design | **Marketing** | Reviews | **Website Content & Design** | Etc.

601 McReynolds Street, Carthage, NC 28327
(910) 947-3189 | contact@donnainkpublications.com

www.donnaink.com

DONNAINK PUBLICATIONS, L.L.C. IS A SMALL, woman-owned, traditional, and "Indie" publishing house with thirty plus authors who arrive from nine countries and five continents to share diverse and eclectic works discriminating readers, derived largely from organic and direct sales growth, love.

Top-ten niche' market bestsellers feature quality representation and presentation. DonnaInk Publications supports copyright in a perceptive ethos inspiring written word innovation while nurturing unique vision and promoting free speech.

We appreciate authorized edition purchases of authors' works and for copyright law compliance; in so doing, readers support writers and publishers' capabilities to publish books every reader enjoys.

This year's motto: Love and Peace in 2021.

Located in Southern Maryland with national and global read.

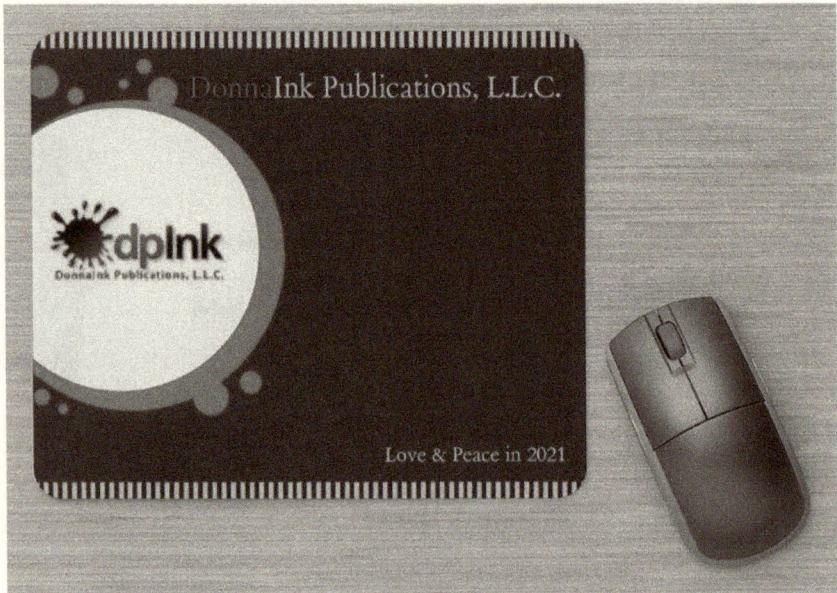

ABOUT THE IMPRINT
BEAT DEEP BOOKS

BEAT DEEP BOOKS IS AN IMPRINT OF DonnaInk Publications, L.L.C. and features entertainment and media works from a variety of authors including Candy Strother DeVore-Mitchell. New works are in production by additional authors within this genre shelf. All our Imprints support one another regarding specific genres where quality layout, design, production, and writing come together to result in enjoyable reading for diverse readers.

Subsequent arts and entertainment titles are indicative of actor, arts, author, book, philanthropists, politics, radio, music, news, writers, etc. who share the commonality of bringing unique life skills to a creative pinnacle where observers are educated, engaged, enthralled, or envisioned . . .

It is our hope as readers the Deep Beat Books Imprint of DonnaInk Publications, L.L.C. brings enjoyment, a smile, and informative reflection to each of you. Enjoy the journey.

ABOUT THE GHOSTWRITER
MS. DONNA L. QUESINBERRY

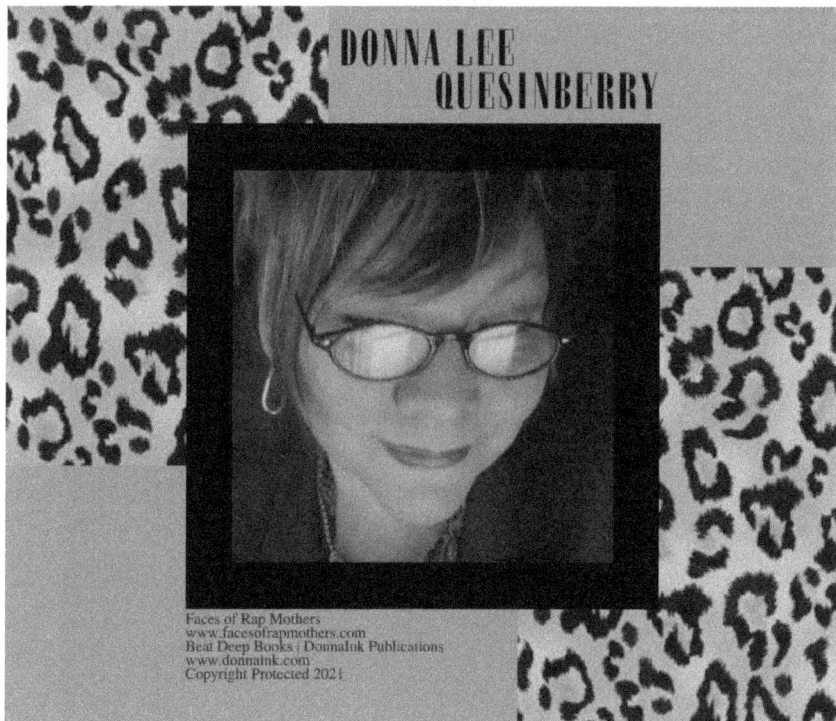

DONNA LEE QUESINBERRY

Faces of Rap Mothers
www.facesofrapmothers.com
Beat Deep Books | DonnaInk Publications
www.donnaink.com
Copyright Protected 2021

MS. DONNA L. QUESINBERRY ("Q") is a powerhouse publisher, ghostwriter, and strategic consultant whose work bridges literary craft with business acumen. As Founder and President of DonnaInk Publications, L.L.C., a woman-owned traditional and indie press, she offers full-spectrum publishing services—including ghostwriting for select clients—through a collaborative, research-driven process that captures each author's authentic voice.

Her editorial approach is immersive and precise, encompassing developmental editing, manuscript architecture, plot refinement, and layout design. Donna also provides brand coaching, image management, and promotional strategy for authors navigating book launches, media appearances, and cross-platform engagement.

In parallel, Donna is Founder and CEO of dpInk Ltd. Liability Company, where she serves as a FedBiz Solutions Expert specializing in business development, capture administration, and proposal architecture. Her solopreneurial arm, ZenCon Arts, supports public relations and creative strategy across entertainment and literary domains.

Academically, Donna holds dual degree accreditation in Business Administration and Computer Science, with a Certificate in International Affairs focused on Eastern Europe and the Middle East. She has completed 500 hours of theological study and has appeared on CNBC, podcasts, and streaming radio.

Donna also serves as President of Faces of Rap Mothers Television Network, COO and CFO of Faces of Rap Mothers Enterprise, and Executive Director/Producer of the DonnaInk Productions Channel. She is an honorary Rap Mother, contributing to a growing media empire that celebrates cultural voices through television, music, and film.

Follow Me Here....

@donnaink

@donnainkpublications

@donnainkpublicatations

@facesofrapmothers

@3036530

@donnaink

FACES OF RAP MOTHERS
FATHERS EDITIONS - BOOK ONE
CANDY STROTHER DEVORE MITCHELL
COMBO
HARD COVER COLOR
Books One thru Four
BOOK FOUR
Candy Strother DeVore Mitchell
BOOK FIVE
CANDY STROTHER DEVORE MITCHELL

FACES OF RAP MOTHERS
SPONSORED MERCHANDISE

Visit https://www.facesofrapmothers to order these and "other" publisher sponsored products – novel items are available with every new title release (e.g.: apparel, jewelry, and other merchandise).

OTHER BOOKS
BY CANDY STROTHER
DEVORE MITCHELL

Rap Mothers®™© Save The Day Series

Book One - 02/13/20

Book Two – 11/30/21

Book Three – 12/31/21

Book Four – TBD

Book Five – TBD

Book Six – TBD

Book Seven – TBD

Book Eight – TBD

Book Nine – TBD

Book Ten – TBD

Faces of Rap Mothers®™© Book Series

Faces of Rap Mothers™ - Book One – 02/13/20

Faces of Rap Mothers™ - Book Two – 10/01/20

Faces of Rap Mothers™ - Book Three – 12/15/20

Faces of Rap Mothers™ - Book Four – 10/31/21

Faces of Rap Mothers™ - Book Five – TBD

Faces of Rap Mothers™ - Book Six – TBD

Faces of Rap Mothers™ - Book Seven – TBD

Faces of Rap Mothers™ - Book Eight – TBD

Faces of Rap Mothers™ - Book Nine – TBD

Faces of Rap Mothers™ - Book Ten – TBD

Faces of Rap Mothers®™© Fathers Editions

Book One – 11/25/21

Book Two – 12/20/21

Book Three – 01/20/22

Book Four – 03/20/22

Book Five – TBD

Book Six – TBD

Book Eight – TBD

Book Nine – TBD

Book Ten – TBD

Faces of Rap Mothers®™© Presents . . .

Group X - Book One – 11/07/21

Curvy Queens of Dallas - Book Two – 03/07/22

Bonnie Williams - Book Three – 07/07/23

Book Four - Forthcoming

Book Five – 01/07/26

Book Six – 06/07/26

Book Seven – 11/07/26

Book Eight – 01/07/27

Book Nine – 06/07/27

Book Ten – 11/07/27

Gimme My

Beat Deep Books

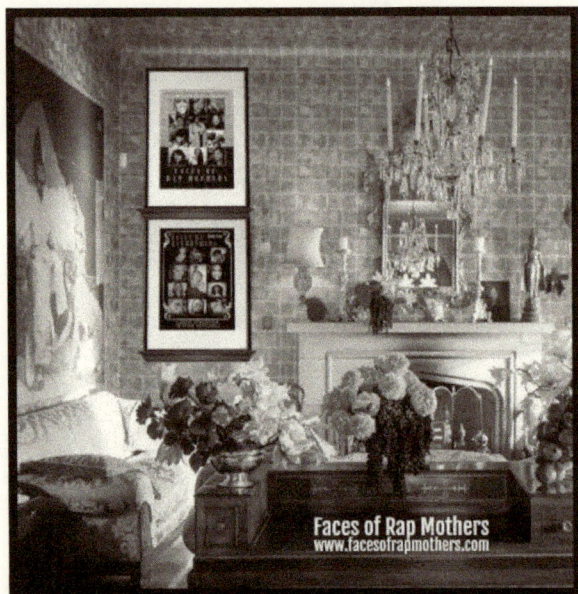

FACES OF RAP MOTHERS
FATHERS EDITIONS - BOOK ONE

CANDY STROTHER DEVORE MITCHELL

Donnaink Publications, L.L.C.

Beat Deep Books
DonnaInk Publications, L.L.C.
17611 Aquasco Road
Brandywine, MD 20613
or
1390 Chain Bridge Road
#10122
McLean, VA 22101
www.donnaink.net | www.donnaink.shop

Email: donnaink@gmail.com

www.ingramcontent.com/pod-product-compliance
Lightning Source LLC
Chambersburg PA
CBHW031430270326
41930CB00007B/642